HEINEMANN GUIDED READERS

UPPER LEVEL

Series Editor: John Milne

Readers at *Upper Level* are intended as an aid to students which will start them on the road to reading unsimplified books in the whole range of English literature. At the same time, the content and language of the Readers at Upper Level are carefully controlled with the following main features:

Information Control As at other levels in the series, information which is vital to the development of a story is carefully presented in the text and then reinforced through the *Points for Understanding* section. Some background references may be unfamiliar to students, but these are explained in the text and in notes in the *Glossary*. Care is taken with pronoun reference.

Structure Control Students can expect to meet those structures covered in any basic English Course. Particularly difficult structures, such as complex nominal groups and embedded clauses, are used sparingly. Clauses and phrases within sentences are carefully balanced and sentence length is limited to a maximum of four clauses in nearly all cases.

Vocabulary Control At Upper Level, there is a basic vocabulary of approximately 2,200 words. At the same time students are given the opportunity to meet new words, including some simple idiomatic and figurative English usages which are clearly explained in the *Glossary*.

Guided Readers at Upper Level

JOHN STEINBECK

Of Mice and Men

Retold by
MARTIN WINKS

Illustrated by
Gay John Galsworthy

HEINEMANN EDUCATIONAL BOOKS
LONDON

Heinemann Educational Books Ltd
22 Bedford Square, London WC1B 3HH
LONDON EDINBURGH MELBOURNE AUCKLAND
HONG KONG SINGAPORE KUALA LUMPUR NEW DELHI
NAIROBI JOHANNESBURG EXETER (NH) IBADAN
KINGSTON PORT OF SPAIN

SBN 0 435 27019 2

First published by William Heinemann in 1966
This retold version for Heinemann Guided Readers
© Martin Winks 1975

This version first published 1975
Reprinted 1976, 1978, 1980, 1983

*Cover photograph by permission of Western Americana
Picture Library*

Printed and bound in Great Britain by
Richard Clay (The Chaucer Press) Ltd,
Bungay, Suffolk

Contents

Glossary

The glossary at the back of this book on page 85 is divided into five sections. A number beside a word in the text, like this [3], refers to a section of the glossary. *Section 1* is only referred to once in the text. Students should note the list of adverbs given in *Section 1* and check on the meanings of any of them about which they are in doubt. Within each section, the words and phrases are listed in alphabetical order.

Section 1 – list of adverbs frequently used in the story
Section 2 – idiomatic phrases
Section 3 – terms to do with life on a ranch
Section 4 – insulting words
Section 5 – other words

ONE

BY THE POOL

Soledad is a town in California. A few miles south of Soledad, the Salinas river forms a deep pool, close to the side of the hill. The water is green, but warm – it has just flowed over the long yellow sands in the hot sun.

On one side of the pool, there are the hills. These hills are the beginning of the Gabilan mountains. On the other side, there are trees and a sandy bank. A path leads through the trees to the water.

One evening, after a hot day, two men came along the path to the pool. They were wearing denim[3] trousers, denim coats and black hats. They were carrying rolled-up blankets on their shoulders. The first man was called George. He was small and quick, with a dark face, restless eyes and a thin nose. The other man was called Lennie. He was a huge man with a large face, pale eyes and wide shoulders.

George stopped by the pool and took off his hat. Lennie dropped his blankets, lay down and started drinking greedily[1] from the pool. George went to him, shook him by the shoulder and said sharply: 'Lennie, don't drink so much. You'll be sick like last night.'

Lennie was still wearing his hat, but he put his whole head under the water, then sat up on the bank and smiled. 'That's good,' he said. 'You drink some, George. Take a good big drink.'

George put his blankets down on the bank. 'I'm not sure it's good water,' he said. 'It looks dirty.'

George knelt down by the pool and drank a little water from his hand. 'It tastes all right,' he said, 'but the water's not running. You shouldn't drink water when it's not moving, Lennie. You don't take enough care.'

George then quickly washed, put his hat on again and sat down on the bank. Lennie watched and then imitated George

exactly. He pulled his hat down over his eyes, just as George had done.

George was in a bad temper. He said angrily: 'That bus driver made us get out at the wrong place. He told us that we would only have to walk a little way down the road to get to the ranch[3]. We must have walked about four miles – on a hot day, too.'

Lennie looked at him and asked nervously: 'George, where are we going?'

'Have you forgotten? Do I have to tell you again?'

'I'm sorry, George. I tried hard not to forget, but I don't remember things easily.'

'O.K.' said George, 'I'll tell you again. Now listen. Listen hard so that we don't get into trouble. Do you remember when we got bus tickets and work cards from the agency[3] in Soledad?'

'Of course I do, George.' Lennie put his hands into his coat pockets. Then he said, 'George, I haven't got my work card, I think I've lost it.'

'You fool, you never had your card. I've got it. Do you think I'd give it to you and let you carry it?'

'I thought I put it in my pocket,' said Lennie, putting his hand in his pocket again.

'What have you just taken out of your pocket?' George asked.

'There's nothing in my pocket,' replied Lennie.

'I know,' said George. 'It's in your hand. What are you hiding?'

'Nothing, George. Honestly.'

'Give it to me.'

Lennie held his closed hand away from George. 'It's only a mouse, George. It's dead. I didn't kill it. I found it dead.'

'Give it to me,' George said again.

'Let me keep it.'

'*Give it to me!*' repeated George angrily.

Lennie slowly handed the mouse to George. George took

the mouse and threw it to the other side of the river. 'Why do you want to keep a dead mouse?' he asked.

'I like stroking it while we are walking along.'

'Well, you're not going to stroke any mice when you're walking with me. Do you remember where we're going now?'

Lennie was embarrassed. He hid his face against his knees and said, 'I've forgotten again.'

'For God's sake! Listen. We're going to work on a ranch. We worked on a ranch in Weed.'

'Weed?' Lennie asked.

'The town in the north,' replied George.

'Oh yes, I remember.'

'The ranch we're going to is a quarter of a mile away,' George continued. 'We're going to see the boss and I'll give him the work cards, but you've got to keep quiet. If the boss finds out how stupid you are, we won't get the job. But if he sees you working first, we'll be O.K. Do you understand?'

'Yes, George, yes.'

'So what are you going to do when we see the boss?'

Lennie concentrated. Then he said, 'I'm going to keep quiet.'

'Good boy,' said George. 'That's fine. Say it two or three times so that you don't forget.'

Lennie repeated quietly: 'I'm going to keep quiet . . . I'm going to keep quiet . . . I'm going to keep quiet.'

'O.K.,' George said, 'And don't do any bad things like in Weed.'

'Like in Weed?' Lennie asked.

'Have you forgotten that too? Well, I'm not going to remind you. I don't want you to do it again.'

Lennie suddenly understood. 'Oh yes, we had to run away from Weed. They didn't catch us. I remember that.'

George lay back on the sand and crossed his hands under his head. Lennie imitated him.

'You're a lot of trouble,' George said. 'If I didn't have you with me all the time, I could have an easier life.'

'We're going to work on a ranch, George,' Lennie said.

'Yes, you know that now. But we're going to sleep here.'

The daylight was quickly disappearing now and the night was coming.

'George, why don't we go to the ranch for supper? We could have supper there.'

'We're going there tomorrow,' said George. 'I like it here.'

'Aren't we going to have any supper?' asked Lennie.

'Of course we are,' said George, 'if you gather some wood for a fire. I've got three cans of beans. Get a fire ready, then we'll heat the beans and have supper.'

Lennie stood up and went away. George lay back on the bank, whistling quietly. 'Poor fool,' he said.

After a minute Lennie came back carrying one small stick of wood in his hand. George sat up. 'All right,' he said sharply, 'give me that mouse.'

'What mouse?' Lennie asked innocently. 'I haven't got a mouse.'

George held his hand out. 'Come on, you're not fooling me. Your feet are wet. I know you've walked across the river to get the mouse back. Give it to me.'

Lennie hesitated and stepped backwards.

'Give me that mouse or I'll hit you,' George said coldly.

Lennie reluctantly put his hand in his pocket. 'Why can't I keep it? It doesn't belong to anybody. I didn't steal it. I found it by the road.'

George was still holding his hand out. Lennie came forward slowly and gave the mouse to him.

Lennie started crying.

'Crying like a baby, a big man like you,' George said. He put his hand round Lennie's shoulder. 'Lennie, I didn't take the mouse from you because I wanted to be cruel. I took the mouse because it wasn't fresh. You stroked it too hard and now it's dead. If you get another mouse that's fresh, I'll let you keep it for a while.'

Lennie sat down on the sand and said miserably, 'I don't

know where there is another mouse. I remember a lady who used to give me mice, but she isn't here now.'

George laughed. 'A lady? Have you forgotten who that was? It was your Aunt Clara. She stopped giving you mice because you always killed them.'

As the two men sat talking, the sun set and darkness came into the valley. A big fish swam up to the surface of the pool to get some air and then disappeared into the dark water again. Rings spread across the water where the fish had been. The wind blew gently through the trees.

'Are you going to get that wood?' George asked. 'There's plenty behind that tree over there. Now go and get it.'

Lennie went to collect wood for the fire.

TWO

SUPPER TIME

After he had lit the fire, George put three cans of beans close to it to heat them. 'We've got enough beans for four men,' he said.

Lennie said, 'I like them with ketchup[5].'

'I've already told you we haven't got any!' George said angrily. 'You always want what we haven't got! If I lived alone I could have a really easy time. I could get a job without any trouble. I could take my pay at the end of every month and go into town to enjoy myself. I could eat what I want, drink whisky, play cards, anything.'

Lennie looked terrified. 'But what have I got?' George continued. 'I've got you. You can't keep a job and I lose every job I get because of you. We have to go all over the country looking for new jobs all the time. You get into trouble, and I have to get you out of it. You fool. You cause trouble for me all the time.

Then George started talking about the girl Lennie had met in Weed.

'You just wanted to touch that girl's dress,' said George. 'You wanted to stroke her dress like stroking a mouse. She didn't know that you only wanted to touch her dress. She tried to move away, but you held her dress as if it was a mouse. She started screaming and we had to run away. We had to hide all day while men were looking for us. It's like that all the time with you. I wish I had a cage with a million mice in it. I'd put you in it and let you have fun.'

George looked across the fire at Lennie. Suddenly he felt ashamed that he had made Lennie feel afraid. Lennie crawled slowly round the fire and sat close to George. George turned the cans of beans so that another side faced the fire.

George looked into the fire. He spoke to Lennie. 'When I think how I could enjoy myself without you, I nearly go mad. I never get any peace with you.'

'George, do you want me to go away and leave you alone?'

'Where would you go?' asked George.

'I could go to the hills over there and find a cave,' replied Lennie.

'Could you? How would you eat? You wouldn't find anything to eat.'

'I'd find things, George.'

George said, 'I was unkind to you just now, Lennie. I was only joking. I want you to stay with me. You always kill mice, so I'll give you a puppy as soon as I can.'

Lennie did not want to think about puppies. 'If you don't want me, just say so. I'll go to those hills over there and live by myself. And nobody will steal mice from me.'

George said, 'I want you to stay with me, Lennie. If you were alone, somebody would think you were a wild animal and shoot you.'

Lennie now began to think about other things. 'George,' he said, 'tell me – like you did before.'

'Tell you what?' asked George.

'About the rabbits,' replied Lennie.

'No, I don't want to.'

'Oh please, George. Tell me – like you did before.'

'O.K., Lennie, I know you love hearing about the rabbits. I'll tell you and then we'll eat our supper.'

George began the story that he had told Lennie many times before. 'Men like us, who work on ranches, are the loneliest men in the world. They have no family and no home. They go to a ranch, work for some money and then go into town and spend it all. Then they go to another ranch to look for more work. They have nothing to think about in the future.'

Lennie was delighted. 'That's it – that's it. Now tell me about us.'

George continued. 'But we're not like those men. We've got something in the future. We've got each other. We can talk to each other and forget other lonely people.'

Lennie interrupted. 'And why? Because I've got you and you've got me and we look after each other. That's why!' He laughed delightedly. 'Go on, George.'

'You know the story by heart.[2] You can tell the story yourself,' said George.

'No. I forget some of the things. Now tell me about the future.'

'O.K.,' replied George. 'Some day we're going to have enough money and we're going to buy a little house with some land, a cow and some pigs and . . .'

'And we're going to live, really live,' Lennie shouted. 'And we're going to have some rabbits. Go on, George! Tell me about the garden and the rabbits in the cages and the rain in winter. Tell me about the stove and the cream on the milk. Tell me, George.'

'Why don't you do it yourself? You know the whole story.'

'No, you tell it, George. It isn't the same if I tell it.'

'All right,' said George. 'We're going to have a big garden for vegetables and some rabbits and some chickens. And when

8

it rains in winter, we'll stop work and make a fire in the stove. We'll sit by the stove, listening to the rain coming down on the roof – oh, I haven't got time to tell you any more.'

George opened two of the cans of beans with his pocket knife and gave one can to Lennie. Then George took two spoons from his side pocket and passed one to Lennie. The two men started eating their supper by the fire.

'What are you going to say tomorrow when the boss asks you questions?' George asked.

Lennie stopped eating and concentrated hard for a few moments. 'I . . . I'm going . . . to keep quiet.'

'Good boy! That's fine, Lennie. Perhaps you're getting better. When we get some land, I can let you look after the rabbits, because you can remember things so well.'

'I can remember,' Lennie said proudly.

'Look, Lennie,' George said. 'I want you to look around you and remember this place. The ranch is about a quarter of a mile away up the river.'

'Yes, I can remember,' replied Lennie. 'I remembered about keeping quiet, so I can remember this place.'

'That's good,' George said. 'Listen, Lennie. If you get into trouble, I want you to come here and hide among the trees.'

'Hide among the trees,' Lennie said slowly.

'Hide among the trees till I come for you,' said George. 'But you aren't going to get into trouble. Remember if you get into trouble, I won't let you look after the rabbits.'

'I won't get into trouble, George. I'm going to keep quiet.'

'O.K.,' said George. 'Bring your blankets. It's going to be nice sleeping here by the fire.'

The two men made their beds on the sand and lay down. The light from the fire grew weaker and the branches of the trees gradually disappeared.

'George,' Lennie called in the darkness. 'Are you asleep?'

'No, what do you want?'

'Let's have different coloured rabbits, George.'

'Of course we will,' George said sleepily. 'Red and blue and green rabbits, Lennie. Millions of them.'

'Furry ones, George, like the ones I saw in Sacramento.'

'Of course, furry ones.'

There was silence for a few moments and then Lennie spoke again.

'If you want, George, I can go away and live in a cave.'

'Don't talk nonsense,' George replied. 'Be quiet now and go to sleep.'

The fire slowly went out and in the distance a dog howled on the other side of the river. The leaves of the trees shook in the gentle wind and the two men slept.

THREE

ARRIVAL AT THE RANCH

The next morning George and Lennie arrived at the ranch. There they met an old man who took them to the bunk-house.

The bunk-house was a long, rectangular building where the ranch workers slept. It had small, square windows in three of its walls and a large wooden door in the fourth wall. Inside, the walls were whitewashed but the floor was un-painted. There were eight bunks against the walls. Five of the bunks had blankets on them, but the other three had only bare sacks of straw as mattresses. Each man had an apple box nailed over his bunk in which he kept little articles such as soap, razors and some of the magazines that ranch workers love to read. There were also some medicines, little bottles and combs. A few ties hung from nails at the sides of the boxes.

Near one wall, there was a black stove with its chimney

going straight up through the ceiling. In the middle of the room, there was a big square table with playing cards spread over it and some boxes for the players to sit on.

The old man went into the bunk-house in front of George and Lennie. He was dressed in blue denim jeans and was carrying a big broom in his left hand.

'The boss was expecting you to arrive last night,' the old man said. 'He was angry when you weren't here to start work this morning.' The old man pointed with his right arm, but there was no hand at the end of it. 'You can have those two beds there near the stove,' he said.

George went over and put his blankets on the bunk. He unrolled his blankets, put his few belongings in the apple box and made his bed neatly with the blankets.

The old man said, 'I think the boss will be here in a minute. He came in this morning when we were having breakfast and said, "Where are those new men?" And he shouted at the stable man, too.'

George sat down. 'The stable man?' he asked.

'Yes,' replied the old man. 'The stable man is black, you see. His name's Crooks. He looks after the horses and cleans the stable. He's a nice fellow[4]. His back's injured where a horse kicked him. The boss always shouts at him when he's angry, but Crooks doesn't care about that. He reads a lot. He's got books in his room.'

'What sort of man is the boss?' George asked.

'Well, he's quite a nice fellow, but he gets rather angry sometimes. Do you know what he did last Christmas? He brought a gallon of whisky in here and said, "Drink and enjoy yourselves, boys, Christmas only comes once a year".'

'Did he really? A whole gallon?' asked George.

'Yes,' continued the old man. 'We had a great time last Christmas. It was a great evening. When the whisky was finished, the others went into Soledad and carried on drinking. But I didn't go; I'm too old for that now.'

Lennie was just finishing making his bed when the door

opened and the boss came in. He was a little man, wearing blue denim jeans, a shirt, a black coat and a brown hat. He also had high-heeled boots to show that he was not an ordinary ranch worker.

The old man walked slowly to the door and said to the boss, 'These men have just come.' Then he went out.

The boss walked forward. 'I wrote to the agency and told them I wanted two men to start work this morning,' he said to George and Lennie. 'Have you got your work cards?'

George took the cards from his pocket and gave them to the boss.

The boss looked at the cards and then at George. 'Why are you late,' he asked. 'It's written here that you should start work this morning.'

George felt embarrassed and looked down at his feet. 'The bus driver told us to get out at the wrong place yesterday. We had to walk ten miles. There was no other bus this morning.'

'Well, you can't start work till after dinner,' the boss replied. He took his time-book [3] out of his pocket and opened it where there was a pencil between the pages. George looked at Lennie, and Lennie nodded to show that he understood about keeping quiet.

'What's your name?' asked the boss.

'George Milton.'

'And what's yours?' said the boss, turning to Lennie.

George said, 'His name's Lennie Small.'

The boss wrote the names in his book. 'Today's the twentieth. You're starting work at noon on the twentieth.' He closed the book. 'Where have you two men been working?'

'Up near Weed,' George said.

'You too?' the boss asked Lennie.

'Yes, he has too,' George answered.

The boss pointed at Lennie and said to George, 'He doesn't talk much, does he?'

'No, he doesn't, but he's a really good worker. He's as strong as a bull.'

Lennie smiled to himself. 'Strong as a bull,' he repeated.

George looked at him angrily and Lennie lowered his head, ashamed that he had spoken.

'Listen, Small!' said the boss suddenly. 'What can you do?'

Lennie hesitated. Then he looked at George for help.

'He can do anything you tell him,' George said. 'Anything you want. Just let him try.'

The boss turned to George. 'Then why don't you let him answer? What are you trying to hide?'

George answered loudly. 'Nothing. He isn't intelligent, that's all. But he's a really hard worker. He can lift a four-hundred pound bale of straw.'

'What's your interest in this man?' the boss asked.

'Nothing,' replied George. 'Why?'

'Well, I've never seen a man take so much trouble for another man. I'd just like to know the reason for your interest.'

George hesitated. 'He's my . . . cousin,' George replied. 'I told his mother I'd take care of him. He was kicked in the head by a horse when he was a child. He's O.K. He's just not intelligent – that's all. But he can do anything you tell him.'

'All right, Milton,' said the boss. 'I'll be watching you, so don't try any tricks because you can't trick me. Go out with the grain teams³ after dinner. They're picking up barley³. Go out with Slim's team.'

'Slim?' George asked.

'Yes,' replied the boss. 'He's a big tall man. You'll see him at dinner.'

The boss went to the door, but, before he went out, he turned and looked at the two men for a long moment.

After the boss had gone away, George was angry with Lennie. 'You were going to keep quiet. You were going to let me talk all the time. We nearly lost the job because of you.'

'I forgot, George,' Lennie replied.

'Yes, you forgot. You always forget, and then I have to get you out of trouble. Now the boss is watching us. Now we've got to be careful. Don't say anything in future. Keep your big mouth shut.'

'George.'

'What do you want now?'

'I wasn't kicked in the head by a horse, was I, George?'

'It would be a good thing if that had happened,' George said harshly. 'Everybody would have less trouble.'

'You said I was your cousin, George.'

'Well, that was a lie. And I'm glad it was. If I was a relative of yours, I'd shoot myself.' George stopped suddenly, went to the open door and looked out. The old man was outside. 'Were you listening to us?' George asked.

The old man came in, carrying his broom and followed by a very old sheep-dog with pale, blind eyes. It struggled to the side of the room, lay down and began licking itself.

'No, I wasn't listening,' the old man said. 'I was just sitting in the shade for a minute with my dog. I'm not interested in anything you were saying. A man on a ranch never listens and he never asks questions.'

'That's right,' George said, satisfied that the old man had heard nothing. 'Come in and sit down for a minute. You've got a very old dog there.'

'Yes, I've had him since he was a puppy. He was a good sheep-dog when he was younger.'

At that moment, a young man with a thin brown face and curly hair came into the bunk-house. He had a glove on his left hand and, like the boss, he was wearing high-heeled boots. 'Have you seen my father?' he asked.

The old man said, 'He was here just a minute ago, Curley. I think he went to the cook-house.'

'I'll go and look for him there,' Curley said.

Curley looked at the new men and stopped. As he looked coldly at George and then at Lennie, his arms slowly bent at the elbows and his hands closed into fists. His body became stiff and he seemed ready to fight. Lennie moved his feet nervously and Curley walked up to him. 'Are you the new men that my father was waiting for?'

'We've just arrived,' George said.

'Let the big man talk,' said Curley.

Lennie twisted his body nervously.

George said, 'Perhaps Lennie doesn't want to talk.'

Curley turned round violently. 'For God's sake, he's got to talk when somebody speaks to him. Why are you interfering?'

'We travel together,' George said coldly.

'I see. And you won't let the big man talk.'

'He can talk if he wants to tell you something,' said George, nodding slightly to Lennie.

'We've just arrived,' Lennie said softly.

Curley stared at Lennie. 'Well, next time answer when somebody speaks to you.'

Curley turned towards the door and walked out, and his elbows were still bent a little.

George said to the old man, 'What's the matter with him? Lennie didn't do anything to him.'

'That's the boss's son,' he said. 'Curley's good with his fists. He's done some boxing.'

'Well, I don't care if he *is* good with his fists,' George said. 'He shouldn't want to fight Lennie. Lennie didn't do anything to him.'

The old man answered. 'Curley's like a lot of little men. He hates big men. He always wants to fight big men. He behaves as if he's angry with them because he isn't a big man. Haven't you met little men like that?'

'Yes, I've seen plenty of them,' George said. 'But Curley had better be careful with Lennie. He's going to get hurt if he tries to start a fight with Lennie. Lennie isn't a fighter, but he's strong and quick and he doesn't know any rules.'

George walked to the square table and sat down on one of the boxes and the old man sat down on another box.

'Curley doesn't care about anybody,' said the old man. 'His

father's the boss so he knows that he'll never lose his job.'

George said, 'This man Curley seems to be a real swine.[4] I don't like cruel, little men.'

'I think he's become worse lately,' the old man said. 'He got married two weeks ago. His wife lives in the boss's house. Curley is more ready to fight since he got married.'

'Perhaps he wants to fight for his wife,' George said.

'Wait till you see her,' said the old man.

'Is she pretty?'

'Yes, she's pretty, but . . .'

'But what?' George asked.

'Well, she's interested in other men.'

'What!' George exclaimed. 'She's been married for two weeks and she's interested in other men already? Maybe that's why Curley wants to fight so much.'

'I've seen her trying to attract Slim, and another time Carlson,' said the old man, standing up. 'Do you know what I think?' George did not answer. 'I think Curley's married . . . a whore.'[4]

'He isn't the first,' George said. 'Plenty of men have married whores.'

The old man moved towards the door, with his old dog following slowly and painfully behind. 'I've got to go now and get the wash-basins ready for the men. The teams will be back soon. Are you going out with Slim's team?'

'Yes,' replied George.

'You won't tell Curley anything I said?' asked the old man.

'Of course not,' replied George.

'Well, just have a look at his wife. You'll see she's a whore.' And the old man went out into the bright sunshine.

FOUR

CURLEY'S WIFE

Outside the bunk-house, George and Lennie heard a horse and waggon arriving at the ranch. 'Crooks, Crooks!' a voice called out in the distance. 'Where's that nigger⁴?'

George listened to Curley shouting, then turned round to look at Lennie, who was lying on his bunk.

'Listen, Lennie,' said George. 'I'm worried. You're going to have trouble with Curley. I've seen men like him before. He thinks you're frightened of him and he's going to hit you soon'.

Lennie looked frightened. 'I don't want any trouble,' he said. 'Don't let him hit me, George.'

George stood up, went to Lennie's bunk and sat down on it.

'I hate that sort of man,' said George. 'I've seen plenty of men like him.' He thought for a moment. 'If he fights you, Lennie, we'll lose our jobs here. That's certain, because he's the boss's son. Look, Lennie, try to keep away from him. Don't speak to him. If he comes in here, go away to the other side of the room. Will you do that, Lennie?'

'I don't want any trouble,' Lennie said miserably. 'I haven't done anything to him.'

'That won't help you if Curley wants to fight you,' George replied. 'Just keep away from him. Will you remember?'

'Of course, George. I'm going to keep quiet.'

The grain teams were just arriving at the ranch for dinner. Outside there was the sound of horses' hooves and waggon wheels, and men were shouting at each other.

Inside the bunk-house, George frowned as he thought about the situation.

'Are you angry with me, George?' Lennie asked.

'Not with you, Lennie,' George answered, 'but I'm angry

with Curley. I hoped we were going to save some money here – maybe a hundred dollars.' He said again, 'Keep away from Curley, Lennie.'

Just then a waggon stopped outside the bunk-house and somebody shouted, 'Crooks, hey, Crooks!'

At that moment both men looked towards the door, because a girl was standing there, looking in. She had a lot of lipstick on her lips and heavy make-up round her eyes. Her finger-nails were painted red and her hair was arranged in little hanging curls. She was wearing a light cotton dress and red shoes with little red feathers on them.

'I'm looking for Curley,' the girl said.

'He was here a minute ago,' George told her, 'but he went away.'

She put her hands behind her back and leaned against the door-frame so that the shape of her body was seen more clearly.

'You're the new men who've just arrived, aren't you?' she asked.

'Yes.'

Lennie looked at the girl's face and body. She did not seem to be looking at Lennie, but she knew that he was watching her.

'Curley sometimes comes in here,' she explained.

'Well, he isn't here now,' said George sharply.

'If he isn't, I suppose I'd better look somewhere else,' she said.

Lennie watched her, fascinated. George said, 'If I see Curley, I'll tell him that you were looking for him.'

The girl smiled and twisted her body proudly. 'There's nothing wrong with looking for somebody,' she said. There were footsteps behind her, going past the bunk-house. She turned her head and said, 'Hello, Slim.'

'Hello, beautiful,' Slim's voice answered.

'I'm trying to find Curley, Slim,' the girl continued.

'Well, you're not trying very hard,' Slim's voice came again.

'I saw him going into your house.'

She suddenly seemed worried. 'Goodbye, boys,' she called into the bunk-house, and hurried away.

George looked at Lennie. 'My God!' he said. 'What a whore! So that's the woman Curley married.'

'She's pretty,' Lennie said.

'Yes, and she likes everybody to see that,' George replied. 'Curley's going to have a hard time with her. I bet she'd run away with any man who paid her twenty dollars.'

Lennie was still staring at the door where she had stood. 'Oh, she's really pretty,' he said and smiled. George turned round to face him, took hold of one of his ears and shook him.

'Listen to me, you fool,' George said fiercely. 'Don't even look at that woman. I don't care what she says and what she does. I've seen dangerous women before, but nobody as dangerous as her. Leave her alone.'

Lennie tried to escape from George's grip. 'I didn't do anything, George,' he said.

'No, you didn't,' George replied. 'But you had a good look at her legs when she was standing there showing them.'

'I didn't mean to do anything wrong, George, honestly.'

'Well, keep away from her,' George said harshly.

'I don't like this place,' Lennie cried out suddenly. 'It's no good here, George. I want to go away.'

'We've got to stay here until we save some money, Lennie,' said George. 'We'll go as soon as we can. I don't like it here either.' He went back to the table and sat down again. 'No, I don't like it. When we've saved a few dollars we'll leave and go and get some work looking for gold.'

'Yes,' Lennie said eagerly. 'Let's go, George, let's go. It's no good here.'

'We've got to stay,' George said sharply. 'Be quiet now. The men are coming.'

FIVE

SLIM'S PUPPIES

From the wash-room near by, George and Lennie could hear the sound of water and wash-basins being filled.

'Perhaps we should go and wash,' George said, 'but we haven't done any work to make us dirty.'

Just then a tall man came to the door of the bunk-house. He was holding his hat under his arm and combing his long, black hair, which was wet from being washed. Like the others, he was wearing blue jeans and a short denim jacket. This was Slim. It was his job to drive the mules which pulled the threshing machine[3] and he was the most skilful worker at the ranch. He could drive ten, sixteen, even twenty mules without anybody helping him. He was a quiet, serious man; everybody respected him and his opinions. Whenever he spoke, he did so slowly and with great understanding, and other men stopped and listened to him. His face did not show how old he was; perhaps he was thirty-five or fifty.

Slim put his hat on and looked kindly at the two men in the bunk-house. 'It's very bright outside,' he said. 'I can't see very well in here. Are you the new men?'

'We've just arrived,' said George.

'Are you going to pick up barley?' asked Slim.

'The boss told us to do that,' George answered.

Slim sat down on a box opposite George. 'I'm glad you're coming into my team,' he said in a gentle voice. 'There are two men in my team who don't work well. Have you ever done this sort of work?'

'Oh yes,' replied George. 'I'm quite good at it, but that big fellow over there,' he said, pointing at Lennie, 'is very good. 'He can pick up more barley than two men working together.'

Lennie smiled at George's words and Slim was pleased that George had praised his friend. 'Do you two men travel around together?' Slim asked in a friendly way, inviting George to tell him more.

'That's right,' said George. 'We look after each other in a way.' Again he pointed at Lennie. 'Lennie isn't intelligent, but he's a really good worker. He's a really nice fellow, but he's just not intelligent, that's all. I've known him for a long time.'

'Not many men travel around together,' said Slim thoughtfully. 'I don't know why. Perhaps people are afraid of each other.'

'It's much nicer to travel around with a man you know,' said George.

As George was speaking, a powerful man with a big stomach came into the bunk-house. His head was still wet from being washed. 'Hello, Slim,' he said, and then he stopped and looked at George and Lennie.

'These men have just arrived,' said Slim.

'I'm glad to meet you,' said the big man. 'My name's Carlson.'

'I'm George Milton, and this is Lennie Small.'

'I'm glad to meet you,' Carlson repeated. Looking at Lennie, he said, 'He isn't very small,' and laughed quietly at his joke. 'No, he isn't small at all.' He turned to Slim. 'By the way, Slim,' he said, 'how's your dog? I didn't see her under your waggon this morning.'

'She had her puppies last night,' Slim answered. 'There were nine of them. I drowned four of them straightaway. She couldn't feed all of them.'

'So she's got five left,' Carlson said.

'That's right,' said Slim. 'I kept the biggest.'

'So she's got five puppies,' Carlson continued. 'Are you going to keep them all?'

'I don't know yet,' replied Slim.

'Well, I've been thinking,' said Carlson. 'Candy's dog is so old he can hardly walk. He stinks, too. Every time he comes into the bunk-house, I can smell him for two days afterwards.

He's nearly blind, he's got no teeth and he can't eat. Candy gives him milk because he can't chew anything else.'

While Carlson was talking, George was looking at Slim and thinking about the five puppies. Suddenly a triangle[3] began to ring outside, slowly at first and then faster and faster.

'It's time to eat,' said Carlson, and outside a group of men went by, talking.

Slim stood up slowly. 'Come on, you men,' he said to George and Lennie. 'There'll be no food left in a couple of minutes.'

Carlson let Slim go out of the door in front of him, and then went out himself.

Lennie looked at George excitedly.

'Yes, Lennie,' George said. 'I heard what Slim said. I'll ask him if you can have one of his puppies.'

'I want a brown and white one,' Lennie shouted in his excitement.

'Come on, let's have dinner,' said George. 'I don't know if Slim's got a brown and white puppy.'

Lennie stayed on his bunk. 'Ask him now, George,' he insisted. 'Ask Slim now, so that he doesn't kill any more of them.'

'O.K. Come on now, stand up.'

Lennie got up from his bunk and the two men walked towards the door. Just then Curley hurried in.

'Have you seen a girl here?' Curley demanded.

'Yes,' said George coldly, 'about half an hour ago.'

'What was she doing here, for God's sake?'

George stood still, watching the angry little man. 'She said she was looking for you,' George replied.

Curley looked at George in a new way, as an opponent in a fight. 'Well, which way did she go?' he asked finally.

'I don't know,' said George. 'I didn't watch her go.'

Curley again looked threateningly at George, then hurried out through the door.

'You know, Lennie,' said George, 'I'm afraid I might

fight that swine Curley myself. My God, I hate him! Come on, let's go to dinner. There'll be nothing left to eat if we don't hurry.'

From a distance there was a sound of rattling dishes and the two friends hurried out to get their dinner.

SIX

LENNIE IN WEED

The same evening, after supper, some of the ranch-workers were playing a game of horseshoes [3] outside in the dying sunshine.

Before the end of the game, Slim and George came into the darkening bunk-house together. Slim went to the table and switched on the electric light hanging over it. The lamp had a simple tin can as a shade, and it threw bright light down on to the table, but left the corners of the bunk-house unlit. Slim sat down on one of the boxes and George sat down on another opposite him.

'It was nothing [2] to give one of the puppies to Lennie,' said Slim. 'I would have had to drown most of them, you know. You don't need to thank me for it.'

'Perhaps it was nothing to you,' said George, 'but it's everything to Lennie. My God, I don't know how we're going to make him sleep in here. He'll want to sleep in the barn with the puppies. It'll be hard stopping him from getting into the box with them!'

'It was nothing,' Slim repeated. 'By the way, what you said about Lennie was absolutely right. Perhaps he isn't intelligent, but I've never seen such a good worker as him. He worked much harder than the other men this afternoon, loading barley on to the waggon. Nobody can work as fast as him.'

'You only have to tell Lennie what to do,' said George proudly. 'He'll do anything, as long as he doesn't have to think how to do it. He can't think how to do things himself, but he always obeys orders.'

They could still hear the other men playing horseshoes outside. The men cheered when one of the players threw a horseshoe and it hit the iron stake.

Slim moved his head away from the table a little so that the light was not on his face. 'It's strange how you and Lennie travel around together,' he said to George, quietly inviting him to talk about Lennie and himself.

'Why is it strange?' George asked suspiciously.

'I don't know really,' Slim replied. 'Hardly any of the men I know travel around together. You know these ranch workers: they arrive, sleep in a bunk here, work for a month and then leave, alone. Nobody seems to care about anybody else. It just seems strange for an idiot[4] like Lennie and a clever little man like you to go around together.'

'Well,' said George. 'Lennie's slow and stupid, but I'm not so clever, either. If I was, I wouldn't come here and load barley for fifty dollars a month with bed and food. If I was clever, I'd have my own little ranch and I'd farm my own crops.'

Slim could feel that George wanted to say more, so he sat quietly, ready to listen.

'It isn't so strange for me and Lennie to go around together,' George continued. 'We were both born in Auburn. I knew his Aunt Clara there. Lennie was put in her care when he was a baby, and she brought him up. When his Aunt Clara died, he started going to work with me. We got used to each other after a while.'

'I see,' said Slim. George looked at him and saw the calm, understanding expression on his face.

'I used to have a lot of fun with Lennie,' George said. 'I used to play jokes on him because he was too stupid to take care of himself.'

27

'I'll tell you why I stopped playing jokes on him,' he continued. 'One day, Lennie and I and some other men were standing by the Sacramento River. I was feeling clever and I wanted to show the others how clever I was. I turned to Lennie and told him to jump into the river. He jumped in, but he couldn't swim and he nearly drowned before we got him out. He was very pleased with me for pulling him out of the water. You see, he just forgot that I'd told him to jump in. I've never done anything like that since then.'

'Lennie's a nice fellow,' said Slim. 'A fellow can be nice without being intelligent. I think sometimes the opposite is true, too. A really clever man is hardly ever nice.'

George picked up the cards on the table and started playing by himself. Outside, the game of horseshoes continued and, although the sun had set, the windows of the bunk-house were still bright.

'Yes, he's a nice fellow,' George said. 'But he gets into trouble all the time because he's so stupid. When we were in Weed . . .' George stopped suddenly as he turned over a card and looked anxiously at Slim. 'You won't tell anybody about it?'

'What did Lennie do in Weed?' Slim asked calmly.

'Well, one day he saw a girl in a red dress,' George said. 'Lennie's so stupid that he always wants to touch everything he likes. He thought the dress was very pretty, so he put his hand out to touch it. The girl was afraid and she screamed. Lennie kept holding the dress because he couldn't think what else to do. The girl screamed more and more because she was so frightened. I heard the noise from where I was standing and I ran to them to see what was happening. Lennie was frightened too, but he didn't know what to do except hold the girl's dress. I hit him on the head with a fence post and he let go. Lennie's terribly strong, you know.'

Slim nodded very slowly. 'What happened then?' he asked.

George continued playing cards as he told his story. 'Well, the girl ran to the police and told them that Lennie had raped[5] her. The men in Weed got a search-party together to look for Lennie. They wanted to hang Lennie without a trial, so we had to hide. We sat in a ditch full of water all day, with only our heads sticking out of the water in the grass at the side of the ditch. Then, when it was dark, we ran away.'

Slim sat in silence for a moment. Then he asked, 'Did Lennie hurt the girl?'

'No, not at all. He just frightened her. I'd be frightened too if Lennie grabbed me. But he didn't hurt her. He just wanted to touch that red dress; it's the same when he wants to stroke those puppies all the time.'

'He isn't nasty,' said Slim. 'I know when a man's nasty.'

'No, of course he isn't, and he does anything I tell him . . .'

George stopped because Lennie had come into the bunkhouse. He was wearing his denim jacket over his shoulders and he walked with his body bent forward slightly.

'Hello, Lennie,' said George. 'How do you like your puppy?'

'He's brown and white – just what I wanted,' said Lennie excitedly. He went straight to his bunk, lay down, turned his face to the wall and drew up his knees towards his chest.

George put his cards down. 'Lennie!' he said sharply.

Lennie turned his head and looked over his shoulder. 'Yes, George, what do you want?'

'I told you not to bring that puppy in here.'

'What do you mean, George? I haven't got a puppy with me.'

George went quickly to Lennie's bunk, pulled his shoulder and rolled him on to his back. Then he picked up the tiny puppy from where Lennie had been hiding him against his stomach.

Lennie sat up quickly. 'Give him to me, George,' he said.

'Get up and take the puppy back to the nest,' George said. 'He's got to sleep with his mother. Do you want to kill him? He was only born last night; he's got to stay in the nest with his mother. Take him back or I'll tell Slim not to let you have him.'

Lennie held out his hands hopefully. 'Give him to me, George,' he said. 'I'll take him back. I didn't mean to do anything wrong, honestly, George. I just wanted to stroke him a little.'

George handed the puppy to Lennie. 'O.K. Take him back quickly, and don't take him out of the nest again. You'll kill him if you aren't careful.'

When Lennie ran out of the bunk-house, Slim was still sitting quietly. His calm eyes followed Lennie out of the door. 'My God,' Slim said. 'He's just like a child, isn't he?'

SEVEN

THE END OF CANDY'S DOG

It was almost dark outside now. Candy came in and went to his bunk, followed slowly by his old dog.

Carlson came in next. He walked to the other end of the bunk-house and switched on the second electric light. He stopped, smelt the air and then looked down at the old dog by Candy's bunk. 'Good God, that dog stinks!' Carlson said. 'Take him out of here, Candy. Nothing smells worse than an old dog. You've got to take him out.'

Candy moved to the edge of his bunk, put his hand down and stroked the old dog. 'I've had him such a long time,' he said. 'I never notice how much he smells.'

'Well, we can't have him in here,' Carlson said, walking over to Candy's bunk and looking down at the dog. 'The smell stays here even after the dog's gone out. He's got no teeth and he's so old that he can hardly move. He's no good to you, Candy, and he's no good to himself. Why don't you shoot him?'

The old man moved around nervously on his bed. 'Good heavens, no! I've had him for so long, since he was a puppy.'

'Look, Candy,' said Carlson. 'This old dog is only suffering all the time. If you took him outside and shot him in the back of the head' – he pointed to the dog's head – 'just there, he wouldn't know what had happened.'

Candy looked around unhappily. 'No,' he said softly, 'I couldn't do that. I've had him too long to shoot him.'

'The dog doesn't have any fun,' Carlson continued, 'and he smells horribly. I know what I'll do. I'll shoot him for you, then you won't have to do it.'

Candy sat up on his bunk and scratched the white whiskers on his cheek nervously. 'I'm so used to him,' he said softly. 'I've had him since he was a puppy.'

'Well, it's just cruel to keep him alive,' said Carlson.

Slim had been watching the old dog with his calm eyes. 'Look,' he said. 'You can have one of my puppies if you want, Candy. Carlson's right. Your dog's no good to himself. I'd be glad if somebody shot me when I was so old that I could hardly move.'

Candy felt helpless after what Slim had said, because everyone respected Slim and his opinions. 'Perhaps it would hurt him if *you* shot him,' Candy said to Carlson. 'I think I'd prefer to kill him myself.'

'You needn't worry,' said Carlson. 'If I shot him, he wouldn't feel anything. I'd put the gun just there.' He pointed to the dog's head with his toe. 'There, at the back of his head. He wouldn't feel anything.'

Candy looked at the other men in the bunk-house, hoping that they would help him to prevent Carlson's plan. No help came. Carlson continued to look down at the animal by Candy's bunk and Candy watched Carlson nervously. Finally Carlson said, 'If you like, I'll shoot the old animal now and that'll be the end of that. There's nothing left for him. He can't eat, he can't see and he can't even walk without feeling pain.'

'You haven't got a gun,' Candy said hopefully.

'Of course I have,' Carlson said. 'I've got a pistol. He won't feel anything.'

'We could do it tomorrow,' said Candy. 'Let's wait till tomorrow.'

'Why should we wait?' asked Carlson and went to his bunk. He pulled his bag from underneath the bunk and took out his pistol. 'Let's do it now,' he said. 'We can't sleep in here with his terrible smell.' He put his pistol in his trouser pocket.

Candy looked at Slim for a long time, hoping that Slim would stop Carlson shooting the dog. Slim did nothing. At last Candy said softly and hopelessly, 'O.K. – take him.' Without even looking at the dog again, he lay back on his bunk, crossed his arms behind his head and stared at the ceiling.

From his pocket Carlson took a thin piece of rope. He bent down and tied it round the old dog's neck. All the men except Candy watched him. 'Come, boy. Come on, boy,' Carlson said softly to the dog. 'He won't feel it,' he said quietly to Candy. Candy did not move or answer. Carlson pulled the rope, again saying, 'Come on, boy.' The old dog stood up slowly and stiffly and followed Carlson towards the door.

Carlson's footsteps died away into the distance and it was silent outside. Silence came into the room, and for a few minutes nobody spoke.

'Would anybody like to play cards?' George asked after a while.

'Yes, I'll play with you,' said a young rancher called Whit, who had come in earlier.

George and Whit sat down opposite each other at the table under the light, but George did nothing to begin the card game. He held the cards in his hands and waited. The room was silent again. Candy lay still, staring at the ceiling. Slim watched him for a moment, then looked down at his hands and put them together.

'For God's sake, why is Carlson taking so long?' Whit suddenly cried out. 'Come on, deal some cards!' he said to George. 'We'll never start the game if we just sit here.'

George held the cards tightly and looked at them, but did nothing. There was silence again.

Then a shot sounded in the distance. The men looked quickly at Candy. Every head turned towards him.

For a moment the old man continued to stare at the ceiling. Then he slowly rolled over, faced the wall and lay silent.

EIGHT

WARNING OF TROUBLE

After Carlson had shot Candy's old dog, the silence disappeared from the bunk-house. George gave some cards to Whit and himself, and they got ready for their game.

Then Whit said, 'You men have really come here to work, then.'

'What do you mean?' asked George.

Whit laughed. 'Well, you've come here on a Friday, and you've got to work tomorrow as well.'

'I still don't understand what you mean,' said George.

Whit laughed again. 'A man who's thinking of taking a job at a ranch usually arrives on Saturday afternoon,' he said. 'He gets supper on Saturday evening and three meals on Sunday. Then, if he doesn't like the place, he can leave on Monday morning after breakfast without doing one minute's work. But you arrived at noon on Friday, so you've got to work for a day and a half, even if you don't like it here.'

George looked honestly at Whit. 'We're going to stay for a while,' he said. 'Lennie and I are going to save some money here.'

The door opened quietly and Crooks' head appeared in the doorway. It was a lean, negro head, with patient eyes and lines on his face caused by pain. 'Mr Slim,' he said.

Slim looked away from Candy towards the door. 'Yes? Oh! Hello, Crooks,' he said. 'What's the matter?'

'Mr Slim,' Crooks said again, 'that big man's playing with your puppies in the barn.'

'Well, he isn't doing any harm,' said Slim. 'I gave him one of them.'

'I just thought I'd tell you,' said Crooks. 'He keeps taking them out of the nest and stroking them. It's not good for them.'

'He won't hurt them,' said Slim.

George looked up from his cards. 'If that big fool's playing around too much,' he said, 'just throw him out, Slim.'

Without answering, Slim followed Crooks out of the room.

Whit picked up his cards and looked at them. 'Have you seen Curley's wife yet?' he asked George.

'Yes, I've seen her.'

'Don't you think she's a whore?' asked Whit.

'I don't know her well enough to say that,' George replied.

Whit put his cards down. 'You only need to stay here and keep your eyes open, and you'll see plenty,' he said. 'She doesn't hide anything. I've never seen a woman like her. She tries to attract all the men here all the time. I bet[2] she does the same with Crooks. I don't know what she wants.'

'Has there been any trouble since she arrived here?' George asked.

It was clear that Whit did not want to play cards now. He wanted to talk about Curley's wife. George took his cards and started to play by himself.

'Curley's very nervous about his wife,' said Whit, 'but we haven't had any trouble yet. Every time the men are here, she appears from somewhere. She always says she's looking for Curley, or that she's looking for something she has lost. I don't think she can keep away from men. Curley can't

35

sit still because of her, but nothing's happened yet.'

'She's going to cause trouble,' said George. 'There's going to be a lot of trouble because of her. She's waiting to catch a man and put him in prison. Curley's going to have a hard time with her. A ranch with a lot of men isn't the right place for a girl to live, especially a girl like her.'

The door opened and Lennie and Carlson came in together. Lennie went quietly to his bunk, hoping that nobody would notice how long he had spent with the puppies. Without looking at Candy, who was still facing the wall, Carlson brought out his bag from under his bunk. From the bag he took a small cleaning rod and a can of oil. He laid them on his bunk, then took his pistol from his pocket and started cleaning it. Candy heard the noise of the pistol being cleaned. He turned over, looked at the gun for a moment and then turned back to the wall again.

'Has Curley been in here yet?' asked Carlson.

'No,' said Whit. 'What's the matter with Curley?'

Carlson looked through the barrel of his gun. 'He's looking for his wife,' he said. 'I saw him going round and round outside.'

'Curley spends half his time looking for her,' Whit said, 'and the rest of the time she's looking for him.'

Curley came into the room excitedly. 'Have any of you men seen my wife?' he demanded.

'She hasn't been here,' Whit answered.

Curley looked round the room threateningly. 'Where's Slim?' he asked.

'He's gone to the barn,' George said.

Curley immediately looked ready to fight. 'When did Slim go to the barn?' he asked.

'About ten minutes ago.'

Curley hurried out and slammed the door behind him.

Whit stood up. 'I think I'd like to see what happens between Curley and Slim,' he said. 'Curley must be really angry if he's thinking of fighting Slim. Curley's good with

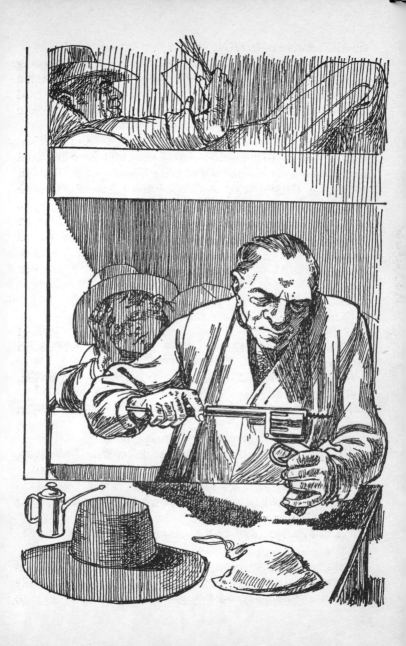

his fists. He's won some boxing competitions, but he'd better leave Slim alone. Nobody knows what Slim can do.'

'Does Curley think that Slim's with his wife?' asked George.

'Yes, he does,' replied Whit. 'Of course, Slim isn't with her, but I'd like to see the fight if it starts. Come on, let's go.'

'I'm staying here,' said George. 'I don't want any trouble. Lennie and I want to stay here and save some money.'

Carlson finished cleaning his gun, put it in his bag and pushed the bag under his bunk. 'I think I'll come out too,' he said. And he followed Whit out of the bunk-house.

NINE

PLANS FOR THE FUTURE

After Whit and Carlson had gone out, George turned to Lennie. 'What are you worried about?' he asked.

'I haven't done anything, George,' Lennie answered. 'Slim told me not to stroke the puppies so much. Slim said it isn't good for them, so I came straight back here. I've been good, George.'

'I told you not to stroke them,' said George.

'Well, I wasn't hurting them,' Lennie replied. 'I was just holding my puppy and stroking him.'

George asked, 'Did you see Slim in the barn?'

'Yes, I did,' said Lennie. 'He told me I'd better not stroke my puppy any more.'

The two men were silent for a few moments. Then George spoke.

'That girl who came in here today – she didn't come into the barn, did she?'

'No, she didn't,' replied Lennie.

George sighed. 'I prefer a good brothel[5],' he said. 'A man can go into a brothel, get drunk and enjoy himself without causing any trouble. He knows how much it's going to cost, too. But Curley's wife – she's nothing but trouble. Somebody will go to prison because of her.'

Lennie thought for a minute and then said, 'George?'

'Yes?'

'George, how long have we got to wait before we can have that little house and some rabbits?'

'I don't know,' said George. 'We'll have to save a lot of money. I know a little ranch that we can buy cheaply, but it still costs money!'

Old Candy turned over slowly. His eyes were wide open, and he watched George carefully, listening to every word.

'Tell me about that ranch,' said Lennie.

'I told you about it last night.'

'Please, George, tell me again.'

'Well, there are ten acres of land,' said George. 'There's a little windmill, a small house and a place for chickens. The ranch has got an orchard too, with different sorts of fruit trees, and a field to grow alfalfa,[3] and there's a river near by . . .'

'And rabbits, George,' said Lennie.

'No, there isn't a place for rabbits yet, but I could easily build one. Then you could feed alfalfa to the rabbits, Lennie.'

'Yes, I could,' said Lennie excitedly. 'That's right, George.'

George's voice became warmer as he spoke about their dream. 'We could have a few pigs too. And when we kill a pig, we could smoke the bacon and ham, and make sausages and things like that. And when the salmon swim up the river, we could catch a hundred of them and salt them or smoke them. We could have salmon for breakfast – there's nothing better than smoked salmon. When the fruit's ripe, we could put it in cans – tomatoes too, they're easy to can. Every Sunday we'd kill a chicken or a rabbit for our dinner. Perhaps we'd have a cow or a goat as well. We'd have fresh milk every day. The cream on the milk would be so thick that you'd have to cut it with a knife.'

Lennie watched George with wide, fascinated eyes, and Candy watched him too. Lennie said softly, 'We could live, really live.'

'That's right,' George continued. 'We'd have all kinds of vegetables in the garden. When we wanted to buy some whisky, we could sell a few eggs or some milk. We'd just live there and it would be ours. We wouldn't have to travel round the country looking for work and eating food cooked by somebody else. No more of that. We'd have our own ranch and it would be our home. We wouldn't have to sleep in a bunk-house.'

'Tell me about the house, George,' Lennie asked.

'O.K. We'd have a little house and a room just for ourselves. There'd be a little iron stove, and in winter we'd have a fire burning all day. We wouldn't have to work more than six or seven hours a day on the land – no more loading barley eleven hours a day. When we planted something, we'd be there to harvest[3] the crop and we'd see the results of our work.'

'And there'd be rabbits,' said Lennie eagerly, 'and I'd take care of them. Tell me how I'd do that, George.'

'All right. You'd go out to the alfalfa field with a sack. You'd fill the sack with alfalfa and take it to the rabbits for them to eat.'

'They'd eat all day,' said Lennie. 'I know how rabbits eat. I've seen them.'

'Every six weeks,' George went on, 'there would be a new lot of baby rabbits, so we'd have plenty of rabbits to eat and sell. And we'd keep a few pigeons that would fly round the windmill.'

Delighted with his description, George stared happily at the wall behind Lennie.

'Everything would be our own,' George continued, 'and nobody could throw us out. If a man came, and we didn't

40

like him, we would say, "Get out," and he'd have to go. And if a friend came to see us, we'd have an extra bunk. We'd ask him, "Would you like to spend the night with us?" and he could stay. We'd have a dog and two cats, but you've got to be careful that the cats don't kill the little rabbits.'

Lennie breathed hard. 'If those cats try to kill the rabbits,' he said angrily, 'I'll break their necks, I'll . . . I'll beat them with a stick.'

Lennie became calm again and talked quietly to himself about the danger of the cats to his rabbits.

When Candy spoke, both George and Lennie looked quickly at each other. Candy said, 'Do you know where there's a ranch like that?'

George was immediately suspicious. 'Perhaps I do,' he said. 'Why do you want to know?'

'You don't need to tell me where it is,' said Candy. 'It could be anywhere.'

'That's right,' said George. 'You could never find it.'

'How much would the owners sell it for?' Candy asked excitedly.

George watched Candy suspiciously. 'Well, I could buy the ranch for six hundred dollars. The old married couple who own it have no money, and the old woman needs to go to hospital for an operation. But why am I telling you this? You've got nothing to do with us.'

'I can't work well with only one hand,' said Candy. 'I lost my right hand here on this ranch. That's why I was given a job as a cleaner here. The boss gave me two hundred and fifty dollars when I lost my hand, and I've saved fifty dollars as well. That makes three hundred dollars. And at the end of the month I'll get my pay – another fifty dollars. Listen . . .' Candy leaned forward eagerly and continued.

'If the three of us bought that ranch together, I could pay three hundred and fifty dollars. I can't do much work, but I'd cook, look after the chickens and do a few jobs in the garden. Would that be O.K.?'

George half closed his eyes, concentrating on this new idea. 'I'll have to think about it,' he said. 'Lennie and I always wanted to buy the ranch by ourselves.'

Candy interrupted him. 'I'd leave my share of the ranch to you two when I die, because I haven't got any relatives. Have you men got any money? Perhaps we could buy the ranch straightaway.'

George spat on the floor, angry that this was not possible. 'Lennie and I have only got ten dollars,' he said. But then he continued, 'Look, if Lennie and I work for a month and spend nothing, we'll have a hundred dollars. With your money we'd have four hundred and fifty. That would be enough to persuade the old people to sell the ranch to us. You and Lennie could go and start living there. I'd get a job somewhere else to earn the rest of the money. While I was working, you could sell eggs and things like that.'

The three men looked at each other, amazed. They had never really believed in this dream. But now the dream was coming true. George said seriously, 'My God, I bet we could do it!' His eyes were full of wonder. 'I bet we could do it,' he repeated softly.

Candy sat on the edge of his bunk, scratching his arm nervously. 'I lost my hand four years ago,' he said. 'I'm sure I'll lose my job here quite soon. Soon the boss will think I'm too old to clean the bunk-house and he'll throw me out. If I give you men my money, perhaps you'll let me do a little work in the garden, even if I don't do it well. I'll wash the dishes and do other small jobs, too. But it'll be our ranch and I'll be working in our own home.'

Candy continued miserably, 'You saw what happened to my dog tonight. Carlson and Slim said he was no good to himself or to anybody else. When the boss throws me out, I'll be like my old dog. I'll have nowhere to go and I shan't be able to get another job. It'll be perfect for me living with you two.'

George stood up. 'We'll do it,' he said. 'We'll buy that

little ranch and go and live there.' He sat down again. They all sat still; all of them were fascinated by the beauty of the idea. And they all thought about the day in the future when the dream would come true.

'When are we going to buy the ranch, George?' asked Lennie.

'In a month,' George replied, 'in exactly one month. Do you know what I'm going to do? I'm going to write to the old people who own the ranch and tell them that we want to buy it. And Candy can send them a hundred dollars.'

Just then, voices were approaching from outside. George said quickly, 'Don't tell anybody about our plans. Let's keep them a secret between the three of us. We'll carry on working here as if we were going to load barley for the rest of our lives. We'll save some money and then one day we'll get our pay and leave.'

Lennie and Candy nodded, both smiling with delight. 'Don't tell anybody,' Lennie said to himself.

'George,' said Candy.

'Yes?'

'I should have shot my dog myself, George,' said the old man. 'I shouldn't have let a stranger shoot my dog.'

TEN

THE FIGHT

The door of the bunk-house opened and Slim came in, followed by Curley, Carlson and Whit. Slim was clearly angry. Curley looked nervous, and was trying to apologise to Slim.

'I didn't mean that you'd done anything wrong, Slim,' said Curley. 'I only asked you if you'd seen my wife.'

'Well, you've been asking me too often lately,' said Slim. 'I'm getting tired of all your questions. If you can't look after your wife, what do you expect me to do about it? Leave me alone!'

'I was just trying to tell you that I didn't mean anything,' said Curley. 'I only thought that you might have seen her.'

'Why don't you tell your wife to stay in your father's house, where she should be?' said Carlson. 'If you keep letting her come into the bunk-house, soon there'll be a lot of trouble.'

Curley turned round to face Carlson. 'Keep out of this, or do you want to come outside and fight?' he said threateningly.

Carlson laughed. 'You stupid little fool,' he said, 'you tried to frighten Slim, but you couldn't do it. Slim frightened you instead. You're a coward. I don't care how good you are at boxing. If you try to fight me, I'll knock your stupid head off!'

Curley looked fiercely at Carlson, but then he stepped back and turned round. He suddenly noticed Lennie, who was still smiling with delight at the thought of the ranch and the rabbits.

Curley ran over to Lennie like a mad dog. 'What are you laughing at?' he asked.

'What?' asked Lennie, unable to understand Curley's sudden anger.

'Come on, you big animal,' Curley shouted. 'Get up and fight. I don't let anybody laugh at me. I'll show you if I'm a coward or not!'

Lennie looked helplessly at George and then he stood up and tried to move backwards. Curley was balanced, ready to fight. He hit Lennie with his left hand, and then punched his nose. Lennie cried out in terror and blood flowed from his nose. 'George,' he cried, 'make him leave me alone.'

Lennie moved backwards until he was against the wall, and Curley followed, hitting him in the face again and again.

Lennie's hands remained at his sides; he was too frightened to defend himself.

George stood up and yelled, 'Get him, Lennie. Don't let him hit you!'

Lennie covered his face with his huge hands. 'Make him stop, George,' he cried helplessly. Then Curley attacked Lennie's stomach and Lennie could not breathe properly.

Slim jumped up. 'Curley's a little swine,' he said. 'I'll fight him myself.'

George put out his hand and held Slim. 'Wait a minute,' he shouted. Then he turned to Lennie and yelled, 'Get him, Lennie!'

Lennie took his hands away from his face and looked around for George, and Curley attacked his eyes. Lennie's big face was covered with blood. 'Get him!' George yelled again.

Curley was just going to hit Lennie again when Lennie grabbed Curley's fist. After a few seconds, Curley was struggling helplessly, and his closed fist was trapped in Lennie's big hand. George ran across to them. 'Let go of him, Lennie,' he shouted. 'Let go!'

But Lennie was terrified now. He watched the struggling little man whom he held, and did not let go. Blood ran down Lennie's face; one of his eyes was cut and closed. George slapped his face again and again, but Lennie still did not let go of Curley's fist. Curley's face went white and his struggling became weak. He started to cry, and his fist remained trapped in Lennie's huge hand.

Again George shouted, 'Let go of his hand, Lennie. Let go! Slim, come and help me.'

Suddenly Lennie let go of Curley's fist and sank down against the wall. 'You told me to get him, George,' he said miserably.

Curley sat down on the floor, looking in amazement at his crushed hand. Slim and Carlson bent over him. Slim looked across at Lennie with horror. 'My God!' he said. 'I think

every bone in Curley's hand is broken.'

'I didn't want to do it,' cried Lennie. 'I didn't want to hurt him.'

'Carlson, get one of the waggons ready,' said Slim. 'We'll take Curley to a doctor in Soledad.'

Carlson hurried out of the bunk-house and Slim turned to Lennie, who was crying softly like a dog.

'It wasn't your fault, Lennie,' said Slim. 'Curley deserves what's happened to him. But my God, his hand's terribly injured.'

Slim hurried out and in a moment returned with a tin cup of water, which he held to Curley's lips. Curley slowly drank a little water.

'Slim, will we lose our jobs now?' George asked. 'We need the money. Will Curley's father throw us out now?'

Slim smiled wisely. He knelt down beside Curley and asked him, 'Are you well enough to listen to me?'

Curley nodded.

'Well, listen,' Slim went on. 'We're going to say that your hand was trapped in a machine. If you don't tell anybody what happened, neither will we. But if you try to have Lennie thrown out, we'll tell everybody what happened.'

'I won't tell anybody,' said Curley. He did not look at Lennie.

The noise of a waggon could be heard outside. Slim helped Curley to stand up. 'Come on,' he said. 'Carlson's going to take you to a doctor.'

Slim took Curley out and the waggon left for Soledad. In a moment Slim came back into the bunk-house. He looked at Lennie, who was still sitting miserably against the wall.

'Let me see your hands, Lennie,' asked Slim.

Lennie showed Slim his huge hands.

'My God!' said Slim. 'I'd hate you to become angry with me.'

'Lennie was just frightened,' said George. 'He didn't know what to do. Nobody should ever try to fight Lennie.'

'That's right,' said Candy seriously. 'You told me that this morning, when Curley first met Lennie.'

George turned to Lennie. 'It wasn't your fault,' he said. 'You don't need to be frightened any more. You only did what I told you to do. You'd better go to the wash-room and wash your face. You look awful.'

Lennie smiled with his bruised mouth. 'I didn't want any trouble,' he said. He walked towards the door, but just before he went out he turned round. 'George?' he asked.

'What do you want?'

'Can I still look after the rabbits, George?'

'Of course you can,' said George. 'You haven't done anything wrong.'

'I didn't want to cause any trouble, George.'

'No, I know,' said George. 'Now go and wash your face.'

ELEVEN

IN THE HARNESS ROOM

Crooks, the stable man, had his bunk in the harness[3] room. This was a little shed next to the barn. On one side there was a small, square window, and on the other there was a narrow door leading into the barn. Crooks' bunk was a long box filled with straw, covered by his blankets. There was an apple box over his bunk, and in the box there were several bottles of medicine, for himself and the horses. Crooks lived alone in the harness room. He could leave his things lying around because he knew that nobody would come in.

He had several pairs of shoes, some rubber boots, a big alarm clock and a shotgun. There were a few books and magazines on a shelf over his bunk. A pair of large spectacles hung from a nail near by.

The room was swept and quite clean because Crooks was a proud man. He avoided meeting other people and he preferred them to leave him alone. His body was bent over to the left because he had an injured back, and his bright eyes were set deep in his head. His lean face was covered with deep black lines, and he had thin lips which showed the pain he felt from his back.

It was Saturday evening, the day after Curley's fight with Lennie. A small electric light was on in the harness room. The door was open and Crooks could hear the horses in the barn moving around quietly and eating their hay.

Crooks was sitting on his bunk, with his shirt pulled out of his jeans at the back. He had a bottle of medicine in one hand. With his other hand, he was rubbing his back to ease the pain that he felt most of the time.

Lennie came silently to the open doorway of the harness room and stood there. For a moment Crooks did not see him, but when he raised his eyes, he immediately became suspicious and frowned. He took his hand away from his back.

Lennie smiled innocently, trying to make friends with Crooks.

'You've got no right to come in here,' Crooks said sharply. 'This is my room. I'm the only one who's got the right to come in.'

Lennie stood there, not knowing what to do. 'Everybody's gone to Soledad,' he said, 'Slim, George and all the others. George told me to stay here and keep out of trouble. I saw your light.'

Lennie took one step into the room. Then he remembered what Crooks had said and stepped back to the door again. 'I've been looking at the puppies,' he said. 'Slim told me not to stroke them so much.'

'You've been taking them out of the nest all the time,' said Crooks. 'I'm surprised that the mother hasn't moved them somewhere else.'

'Oh, she doesn't mind. She lets me stroke them,' said Lennie, moving into the room again.

Crooks frowned, but Lennie was smiling again.

'I can see that you're not going to leave me alone,' Crooks said, 'so come in and sit down for a while.' His voice was more friendly. 'Did you say all the men have gone into town?'

'All except old Candy,' Lennie replied. 'He's sitting in the bunk-house – he's thinking.'

'Thinking?' asked Crooks. 'What's Candy thinking about?'

'About the rabbits!' Lennie exclaimed.

'You're mad,' said Crooks, 'absolutely mad. Which rabbits are you talking about?'

'The rabbits that we're going to get. I'm going to look after them, cut grass and give them water.'

'You're absolutely mad,' Crooks repeated.

'It's true,' said Lennie quietly. 'We're going to do it. We're going to get a little ranch and live there, really live.'

Crooks moved around on his bunk to make himself more comfortable. 'Sit down,' he said in a friendly voice.

Lennie sat down near Crooks' bunk. 'You think it's a lie,' he said, 'but it's true. Every word's the truth. You can ask George if you like.'

'Is George the man you travel with?' asked Crooks.

'That's right. We go everywhere together.'

'You're lucky,' Crooks continued. 'You've got somebody who goes around with you and talks to you. I've got nobody. I was born here in California. My father had a chicken ranch with about ten acres of land. There wasn't another black family for miles around. Now I'm the only black man on this ranch and there's only one negro family in Soledad.' He laughed a little at his loneliness. 'I've got nobody to talk to. If I say something, the other men don't listen because I'm just a nigger.'

Lennie asked, 'How long do you think it'll be before I can stroke the puppies?'

Crooks laughed again. 'You forget everything,' he said.

'A man can talk to you and know that you won't tell anybody any secrets. It'll be O.K. to stroke the puppies in a couple of weeks.'

Crooks leaned forward excitedly, trying to make Lennie understand the difference between them. 'I'm just a nigger,' he continued, 'a nigger with an injured back, and nobody cares about me. You've got George and he talks to you, even if you forget what he says. He's with you all the time and he looks after you, but I've got nobody.'

Crooks paused and Lennie remained silent. Crooks spoke again, softly this time.

'Suppose George doesn't come back from town tonight,' he said, 'and you never see him again.'

'He won't do that,' Lennie cried. 'George wouldn't do anything like that. I've been with George for a long time. He'll come back tonight.'

'You've got George,' said Crooks softly. 'You know he's going to come back. But look at me. I've got nobody. I can't go into the bunk-house and play cards because I'm black. How would you like to be me? I have to sit here and read books. Oh yes, I can play horseshoes until it's dark, but then I have to read books in here. Books are no good. A man needs somebody to be with him and near him.'

Lennie was not listening to Crooks' sad story. He was thinking about George. 'George is going to come back,' he said to himself. 'Perhaps George has come back already. Maybe I should go and see if he's in the bunk-house.'

Crooks continued quietly. 'I remember when I was a child on my father's chicken ranch. I had two brothers. They were always near me, always there. We used to sleep in the same room, in the same bed. We had strawberries in the garden and an alfalfa field. I used to take the chickens out to the alfalfa field on sunny mornings.'

Crooks was now talking about something that Lennie could understand. 'George says that we're going to have alfalfa for the rabbits,' he said.

'Which rabbits?'

'We're going to have rabbits and strawberries,' said Lennie.

'You're mad,' said Crooks.

'It's true. You can ask George.'

'You're mad,' Crooks repeated sharply. 'I've seen hundreds of men arriving at this ranch with their rolled-up blankets on their backs, hundreds of them. They all think about owning a ranch. But they never get what they want. The ranch is just a dream; they never get it.'

Crooks paused and looked towards the door because the horses were moving restlessly. 'I think there's somebody in the barn,' he said. 'Perhaps it's Slim. Slim sometimes comes into the barn two or three times a night. He's a really good worker and he takes good care of his animals.'

Crooks stood up, again feeling pain from his back, and moved towards the door. 'Is that you, Slim?' he called.

Candy's voice answered. 'Slim's gone into town. Have you seen Lennie?'

'Do you mean the big man?' asked Crooks.

'Yes. Have you seen him?'

'He's in here,' Crooks answered. He went back to his bunk and lay down.

Candy appeared in the doorway, scratching his arm and looking into the harness room. He did not try to enter. 'I say, Lennie,' he said, 'I've been thinking about those rabbits.'

'You can come in if you want,' Crooks said reluctantly.

Candy seemed embarrassed at the idea of going into Crooks' room. 'I don't know,' he said. 'But . . . if you want me to.'

'Come in,' said Crooks. 'If everybody's going to come in, you can come too.' He was pleased to have so many visitors although he was trying to appear angry.

Candy came in, but he was still embarrassed. 'This is a nice little room,' he said to Crooks. 'You must be glad to have a room just for yourself.'

'You were going to tell me about the rabbits,' said Lennie, interrupting.

Candy leaned against the wall and continued to scratch his arm where his hand had been. 'I've been here a long time,' he said, 'and so has Crooks. But this is the first time I've ever been in Crooks' room.'

'Men don't come into a black man's room very much,' said Crooks miserably. 'Only Slim and the boss have been in here.'

Candy quickly changed the conversation. He did not want to talk about the differences between blacks and whites. 'Slim's the best worker I've ever met,' he said.

Lennie leaned towards the old man. 'What about the rabbits?' he asked again.

Candy smiled. 'I've worked out a plan,' he said. 'We can make some money with the rabbits if we know how to organise things.'

'But I'm going to look after the rabbits,' Lennie interrupted. 'George said I could look after them. He promised.'

Now it was Crooks' turn to interrupt. 'You men are fooling yourselves,' he said. 'You'll talk about the ranch a lot, but you'll never get it. You'll be a cleaner here till you die, Candy. I've seen too many men with ideas like yours. Lennie will work for two or three weeks, but then he'll leave and travel around looking for work again. Everybody seems to think about owning land, but nobody ever gets it.'

Candy rubbed his cheek angrily. 'We're going to get that ranch,' he said. 'George says we're going to do it. We've got the money ready.'

'Really?' said Crooks. 'And where's George now? He's in Soledad in a brothel. He's spending your money. My God, I've seen it happen so many times. I've seen too many men who wanted to own land, but they never got any.'

'Of course men want to own land,' cried Candy. 'Everybody wants a little bit of land that belongs to him. Every man wants to have somewhere to live, where nobody can throw him out. I've never had anything like that. I've planted crops on a lot of ranches in California, but they weren't my crops. When we harvested them it wasn't my harvest. But we're going to do it now. George hasn't got the money with him in Soledad. The money's in the bank. The ranch is going to be for me and Lennie and George. We're going to have a room for ourselves, and a dog and some rabbits and some chickens. We're going to have green corn, and maybe a cow or a goat as well.' He stopped, fascinated by his description.

'Did you say you've got the money?' Crooks asked.

'That's right,' said Candy. 'We've got most of the money. We'll have it all in a month. George has already chosen the ranch.'

Crooks put his hand behind him and felt his back. He hesitated. '. . . If you . . . men . . . wanted somebody to come and work for nothing, I'd come and help you. I don't need money, only a bed and food. I've got an injured back, but I can still work very hard if I want to.'

TWELVE

ANOTHER VISITOR FOR CROOKS

As Crooks was saying how well he could work, a woman's voice interrupted the conversation.

'Have any of you men seen Curley?'

Candy, Lennie and Crooks turned round to look at the door. Curley's wife was standing there, looking in. She had a lot of make-up on her face, and her lips were slightly parted. She was breathing quickly, as though she had been running.

'Curley hasn't been here,' said Candy coldly.

Curley's wife remained by the door, smiling a little at the three men. She looked at them all in turn. 'I can see that the other men have left all the weak ones here,' she said finally. 'And I know where they all went – Curley, too. I know where they all are.'

Lennie watched her, fascinated, but Candy and Crooks felt embarrassed and avoided her eyes.

After a pause, Crooks said, 'Perhaps you should go back to your own house now. We don't want any trouble.'

'Well, I'm not giving you any trouble,' the girl said. 'I like talking to somebody now and then. Do you think I like staying in that house all the time?'

'You've got a husband,' Candy said harshly. 'You shouldn't keep trying to talk to other men. You're causing trouble.'

The girl became angry. 'Of course I've got a husband,' she said. 'You've all seen him. What a husband! He spends all his time saying he's going to hit someone. I have to stay in that little house and listen to Curley telling me how he's going to fight somebody.'

She paused, and became calm again. 'By the way, what happened to Curley's hand?' she asked.

There was an embarrassed silence. Candy looked quickly at Lennie and then said, 'Oh . . . Curley . . . his hand was trapped in a machine. That's how it was injured.'

The girl looked at Candy for a moment, then laughed. 'Rubbish!' she exclaimed. 'What are you trying to tell me? Curley started a fight with someone, but he chose the wrong person. Trapped in a machine – rubbish! He hasn't done any fighting since it happened. Who did it to him?'

'His hand was trapped in a machine,' Candy repeated.

'All right,' she said coldly. 'Do you think I care? You think you're very clever, but you're tramps[4], all of you. Do you think I'm only a child who knows nothing? I know plenty. I could have been an actress, and a film producer once told me I could be in films . . .' She was now breathing heavily with anger. 'Saturday night! Everybody's gone out to have a good time, everybody! And what am I doing? I'm standing here talking to three tramps – a nigger, an idiot and a stupid old man. I'm even enjoying it because there's nobody else here!'

Lennie watched her, his mouth half open. Crooks had become silent. But Candy's attitude changed. He stood up suddenly.

'I've had enough,' said Candy angrily. 'We don't want you here. We told you that. I'll tell you something else too. You've got the wrong idea about us. You haven't got enough sense to see that we aren't fools. Suppose we lose our jobs because of you. You think we'll travel around and look for another miserable job like this one. Well, you're wrong. You don't know that we're going to get our own ranch. We don't need to stay here. We've got a house and some chickens and some fruit trees – a place a hundred times better than this ranch. We've got friends as well, real friends. We don't need to be afraid of losing our jobs any more. We've got our own land, it's ours, and we can go there.'

Curley's wife laughed at the old man. 'Rubbish!' she said. 'I've seen too many men like you. If you only had fifty cents, you'd spend it all on whisky. I know what sort of men you are.'

Candy's face had become redder and redder with anger. But before Curley's wife had finished speaking, he controlled his anger and continued in a quiet voice.

'I knew you would say something like that,' Candy said to the girl gently. 'Perhaps you'd better go away now and leave us alone. We've got nothing to say to you at all. We know what we've got, and we don't care whether you believe us or not. I think you should leave us now, because Curley might not like his wife to be in the barn talking to "tramps".'

She looked from one face to the other, but they were all unfriendly. She looked longest at Lennie, until he lowered his eyes in embarrassment. Suddenly she said, 'Where did you get those bruises on your face?'

Lennie looked up nervously. 'Who – me?' he asked.

'Yes, you.'

Lennie looked at Candy for help and then he looked down again. 'Curley's hand was trapped in a machine,' he said.

Curley's wife laughed. 'I see; so you're the machine,' she said. 'I'll talk to you later. I like machines.'

Candy interrupted. 'Leave this man alone,' he said. 'Don't try to do anything to him. I'm going to tell George what you've said. George won't let you do anything to Lennie.'

'Who's George?' she asked Lennie. 'Is he the little man you arrived with?'

Lennie smiled happily. 'That's right,' he said. 'That's George, and he's going to let me look after the rabbits.'

'Well, if you like rabbits so much,' said the girl kindly, 'I might get some for you.'

Crooks stood up from his bunk. 'I've had enough,' he said coldly to the girl. 'You've got no right to come into a black man's room. You've go no right to be in here at all. Now get out, quickly. If you don't, I'm going to ask the boss not to let you come into the barn again.'

She turned to Crooks in anger. 'Listen, nigger,' she said. 'Do you know what I can do if you talk to anybody?'

Curley's wife moved towards Crooks. 'Do you know what I could do?' she repeated, pushing Crooks against the wall.

Crooks seemed to grow smaller, and he pressed himself closer against the wall. 'Yes,' he said quietly.

'Well, remember who you are, nigger,' she said. 'You're a black stable man and I'm the wife of your boss's son. I could very easily have you hanged; very easily!'

Crooks did not say anything to continue the argument. He simply repeated, 'Yes,' even more quietly.

For a moment, Curley's wife stood over him. It looked as if she was waiting for Crooks to move so that she could hit him. But Crooks sat still, looking down silently. Finally she turned to the other two men.

Old Candy was watching her, amazed by her anger. 'If you tried to get Crooks hanged,' he said sharply, 'we'd tell everybody what really happened.'

'You can tell whoever you like!' she cried. 'Nobody would listen to you. You know that!'

Candy realised that she was right. 'No,' he agreed. 'Nobody would listen to us.'

'I wish George was here,' Lennie whispered. 'Oh, I wish George was here.'

Candy walked over to him. 'Don't worry, Lennie,' he said. 'I heard the men coming back just now. I bet George is in the bunk-house already.' He turned to Curley's wife. 'You'd better go home now,' Candy said quietly. 'If you go now, we won't tell Curley you were here.'

The girl looked suspiciously at Candy. 'I'm not sure that you heard the men coming back,' she said.

'If you're not sure,' said Candy, 'you'd better do the safest thing and go now.'

She turned to Lennie. 'I'm glad you hurt Curley,' she said. 'He deserved it. Sometimes I'd like to hit him myself.'

She went out of the door and disappeared into the dark barn.

Crooks was the first to speak after the girl had gone. 'Were you telling the truth when you said that the men had come back?' he asked Candy.

'Of course; I heard them,' Candy replied.

'Well, I didn't hear anything,' said Crooks.

'I heard somebody closing the gate,' Candy explained.

In the barn the horses moved around and their chains rattled. A voice called, 'Lennie. Oh, Lennie. Are you in the barn?'

'It's George,' Lennie cried. 'Here, George,' he answered. 'I'm in here.'

In a moment George was standing at the door. He looked in with an angry expression on his face. 'What are you doing in Crooks' room?' he asked Lennie. 'You shouldn't be here.'

Crooks nodded and said, 'I told Lennie that, but he still came in.'

'Well, why didn't you throw him out?' asked George.

'I didn't mind really,' said Crooks. 'Lennie's a nice fellow.'

Now Candy began to think about the future again. 'Oh, George,' he said, 'I've been thinking a lot. I've worked out how we can make some money with the rabbits.'

George frowned. 'I told you not to tell anyone,' he said.

'I only told Crooks,' said Candy, disappointed by George's words, 'I didn't tell anybody else.'

'Well, get out of here, you two,' George ordered. 'My God, I think you'd do something wrong if I left you just for a minute.'

Candy and Lennie stood up and went towards the door. Crooks called, 'Candy!'

'Yes?' Candy replied.

'Do you remember what I said about coming and helping you?' asked Crooks.

'Yes,' said Candy, 'I remember.'

'Well, just forget it. I didn't mean it, I was only talking. I wouldn't want to go to a place like that.'

'O.K.,' said Candy, 'You needn't come if you don't want to. Goodnight.'

The three men went out of the door and they walked through the barn, past the horses, to the bunk-house.

Crooks sat on his bunk and looked at the door for a moment. Then he reached for the bottle of medicine. He pulled his shirt out of his jeans, poured a little of the medicine into his hand and slowly started rubbing his back.

THIRTEEN

DEATH IN THE BARN

The next afternoon was hot and sunny. As it was Sunday, the men did not have to work and a lot of them were playing horseshoes near the bunk-house.

In the barn it was quieter; the resting horses were chewing hay and rattling their chains gently. Flies were buzzing through the warm air and the sun was shining through the cracks of the barn walls.

One end of the barn was piled high with new hay. At the other end, Lennie was sitting alone in the hay. Beside him was the wooden box which was the puppies' nest. Lennie was looking at a little dead puppy which was lying in front of him. He looked at it for a long time. Then he put out his huge hand and stroked the puppy from one end of its body to the other.

'Why did you have to die?' Lennie said softly. 'You aren't as little as mice. I didn't press your head very hard.' He bent the puppy's head up and looked at its face. Then he said to it, 'Maybe George won't let me look after the rabbits now if he finds out that you're dead.'

He made a little hole in the hay, laid the puppy in it and covered it with a pile of hay. But he continued to stare at the pile that he had made.

At that moment, Curley's wife came into the barn. She entered quietly so that Lennie did not see her at first. She was wearing her light cotton dress and the shoes with the little red feathers. Her face was made up and the little hanging curls were all tidy. She was quite near to Lennie before he looked up and saw her.

Lennie was frightened and he covered the dead puppy with more hay.

'What have you got there, young man?' she asked.

Lennie looked down at the hay. 'George says I mustn't talk to you,' he said.

Curley's wife laughed and knelt in the hay next to him. 'Listen,' she said. 'All the men are having a horseshoe competition outside. It's only about four o'clock. Nobody's going to leave the competition before it finishes. Why can't I talk to you? I never get the chance to talk to anybody. I get terribly lonely.'

'Well, I'm not supposed to talk to you,' said Lennie. 'George is afraid I'll get into trouble.'

'What have you got in the hay there?' she asked, changing the conversation.

'Just my puppy,' he said sadly, and he moved the hay so that the girl could see it.

'Oh, he's dead,' she cried.

'He was so little,' said Lennie. 'I was just playing with him. I thought he was going to bite me. I pressed his head a little . . . and . . . and he was dead.'

'Don't worry,' said Curley's wife kindly. 'You can get another one.'

'Yes, I know,' Lennie continued miserably, 'but now George won't let me look after the rabbits.'

'Why won't he?'

'Well, he said that if I do any more bad things, he won't let me look after the rabbits.'

She moved closer to Lennie and spoke kindly again. 'Don't worry about talking to me. Can you hear the men shouting outside? They're playing for money and nobody will leave till the competition is over.'

'If George sees me talking to you,' Lennie said nervously, 'he'll become angry with me. He told me that.'

Her face grew angry. 'What's the matter with me?' she cried. 'Can't I talk to anybody? You're a nice fellow. Why shouldn't I talk to you? I'm not doing anything wrong to you.'

'Well, George says you'll get us into trouble.'

'Oh, rubbish!' she exclaimed. 'What am I doing wrong

now? Nobody here cares about my life. I'm not used to living like this. I could have done something better with my life.' She added thoughtfully, 'Maybe I will, one day.'

Then she started to tell Lennie about her life. She talked quickly. 'I come from Salinas, not far from Soledad,' she said. 'One day a travelling theatre came to the town and I met one of the actors. He told me that I could travel with them. But my mother wouldn't let me go because I was only fifteen. If I *had* gone, I wouldn't be living like this, believe me.'

Lennie stroked the dead puppy again. 'We're going to have a little ranch – and rabbits,' he explained.

The girl continued her story quickly before Lennie could interrupt her again. 'Another time I met a man who worked in films. I went dancing with him. He said that I could be a good actress. He promised to write to me as soon as he got back to Hollywood.' She looked carefully at Lennie to see if he was listening.

'I never got that letter,' she continued. 'I think my mother stole it. I asked her if she'd taken it, but she said she hadn't. Well, I didn't want to stay in Salinas, so I married Curley. I met him when I was out dancing . . . Are you listening?'

'Me?' said Lennie. 'Yes, of course.'

'Well, I haven't told anybody about this before,' the girl went on. 'Perhaps I shouldn't. I don't like Curley; I really don't.'

Because she had told Lennie one of her secrets, she again moved closer to him and was now sitting next to him. 'I could have been in films and worn lovely clothes like those famous film stars,' she continued. 'I could have sat in those big hotels in Hollywood, and people would have taken photographs of me. I could have gone to film shows without paying for a ticket because I would have been one of the actresses. Oh, those lovely clothes – and that man said I could have been a great actress.'

She looked up at Lennie and made a gentle movement with her hand and arm to show that she could act.

Lennie sighed heavily. From outside came the noise of a horseshoe hitting the iron stake and the men cheering. As the sun went down, the light shone through the cracks and climbed up the barn walls, over the heads of the horses.

Lennie said, 'Maybe if I took this puppy outside and threw him away, George would never know that I'd killed him. Then I could look after the rabbits without any trouble.'

Curley's wife said angrily, 'Don't you think about anything except rabbits?'

'We're going to have a little ranch,' Lennie explained proudly. 'We're going to have a house and a garden and an alfalfa field. The alfalfa is for the rabbits.'

'Why do you like rabbits so much?' the girl asked.

Lennie had to think before he could answer this question. He carefully moved nearer to her until they were sitting very close together. 'I like stroking nice things,' he said. 'Once I saw one of those long-haired rabbits. They were really nice. Sometimes I stroke mice, but not when I can get something better.'

Curley's wife moved away from him a little. 'I think you're mad,' she said.

'No, I'm not,' Lennie explained seriously. 'George says I'm not. I like to stroke nice, soft things with my fingers.'

The girl felt more relaxed again and she smiled at Lennie. 'You're mad,' she said, 'but you're a nice fellow in a way. You're just like a big baby. I can understand what you're talking about, though. When I'm brushing my hair, sometimes I just sit and stroke it because it's so soft.'

She ran her fingers over the top of her head. 'Some people's hair isn't soft,' she continued, 'and Curley's hair is just like wire. But mine is soft and fine. I brush it a lot, you see, and that makes it fine. Here – feel it just here.' She took Lennie's hand and put it on her head. 'Feel it there and see how soft it is.'

Lennie's big hands started stroking her hair.

'Don't make it untidy,' she said.

'Oh! That's nice,' said Lennie, and he stroked harder. 'Oh, that's nice.'

'Be careful, you'll make it untidy,' the girl repeated, and then she cried angrily, 'Stop now. You'll make my hair all untidy.' She moved her head quickly and Lennie grabbed her hair and held it tightly.

'Let go!' she screamed. 'Let go!'

Lennie was frightened by the girl's scream and his face was twisted with fear. The girl screamed again, and Lennie put his other hand over her mouth and nose.

'Please don't yell,' he begged. 'George will be angry.'

She struggled violently and tried to scream for help, but Lennie's hand prevented her from making much noise. Lennie began to cry with fear. 'Oh, please don't yell,' he said again. 'George will say that I've done a bad thing. He won't let me look after the rabbits.'

Lennie moved his hand a little and the girl's screaming became loud again. Then Lennie grew angry. 'Don't!' he said. 'I don't want you to yell. You'll get me into trouble; George said you would get me into trouble. Now stop it!'

She continued to struggle, and her eyes were filled with terror. Lennie shook her angrily. 'Don't yell,' he said, and shook her again. Her body jumped suddenly and then she lay still. Lennie had broken her neck, and she was dead.

He stood up and looked down at her. Then he carefully took his hand away from her mouth. She lay still.

'I don't want to hurt you,' he said, 'but George will be angry if you yell.' When she neither answered nor moved, he bent down over her. He lifted her arm and let it drop. For a moment he seemed confused. Then he whispered in fear, 'I've done a bad thing. I've done another bad thing.'

He moved some of the hay with his hands and partly covered her with it.

From outside came the sound of men shouting and cheering. Now Lennie remembered where he was and who was outside. He stood still and listened. It seemed that nobody had heard what had happened in the barn.

'I've done a really bad thing,' he said. 'I shouldn't have done that. George is going to be angry. He told me to hide in the trees till he comes. That's what he told me to do if I was in trouble.'

Lennie looked at the dead girl again. The puppy was lying close to her. Lennie picked it up. 'I'll throw him away,' he said. 'I've got enough trouble.'

Lennie put the puppy under his coat, crept to the barn wall and looked out between the cracks. Then he crept to the door of the barn and went out.

The sun was shining high up on the walls now, and the light was growing soft in the barn. Curley's wife was lying on her back, and she was half covered with hay.

FOURTEEN

WHAT WILL HAPPEN TO LENNIE?

After Lennie had gone away, it was very quiet in the barn. Even the noise of the horseshoe game seemed to grow quieter. In the barn it was getting dark although it was still bright outside. The puppies' mother, a shepherd dog, came in. The smell of Curley's dead wife came to the dog's nose, and the hair rose along her back. She made a noise and hurried to the wooden box, where she jumped in among the puppies.

The body of Curley's wife lay half covered with yellow hay. Now her face seemed different. The unhappiness and the ambition had all disappeared. Now she was very pretty and simple, and her face was sweet and young. The make-up on her cheeks and lips made her look as if she was alive and asleep. The curls of her hair were spread on the hay behind her, and her lips were parted.

The peace was broken by old Candy's voice as he came into the barn. 'Lennie,' he called. 'Oh, Lennie! Are you in here? I've been thinking about the ranch again, and I'll tell you what we can do.'

Candy came closer to the dead body. 'Oh, Lennie!' he called again, and then he stopped. He had noticed Curley's wife. His body stiffened and he rubbed the side of his arm on his face. 'I didn't know you were here,' he said to her.

When the girl did not answer, Candy stepped nearer. 'You shouldn't be here,' he said. 'You should be at home.'

Candy suddenly realised that something was wrong. He moved even nearer to her. 'Oh,' he cried. He looked around helplessly and rubbed his face. Then he jumped up and went quickly out of the barn.

In a moment Candy came back with George.

'What do you want to tell me?' asked George.

Candy pointed at Curley's wife. George stared at her. 'What's the matter with her?' he asked. Then he stepped closer. He knelt down beside her and put his hand over her heart. After a while he stood up slowly and stiffly, his face and eyes hard and cold.

Candy said, 'How did it happen?'

George looked coldly at him. 'Don't you know?' he asked, and Candy was silent. 'I should have known that this would happen,' George said helplessly. 'Perhaps I did know, really.'

'What are we going to do now, George?' asked Candy. 'What are we going to do now?'

George took a long time to answer. 'I suppose . . . we've got to tell . . . the men. I suppose we've got to find Lennie and put him in prison. We can't let him get away. The poor fool would starve.' George tried to imagine Lennie's future. 'Maybe he'll be put in prison and treated kindly.'

But Candy said excitedly, 'We ought to let him get away. You don't know Curley very well. Curley will want to have Lennie hanged. Curley will make sure he's hanged.'

George looked at Candy. 'Yes,' he said at last. 'You're right; Curley will do that. So will the other men.' George looked down again at Curley's wife.

Then Candy spoke about his greatest fear, his fear about the future. 'You and I can buy that little ranch, can't we, George? You and I can go there and live well, can't we, George? Can't we?'

Before George answered, Candy lowered his head and looked at the hay. He knew the answer.

George said softly, 'I think I knew all the time that it was impossible. I knew we'd never buy that ranch, but Lennie liked hearing about it so much.'

'Then – is that the end of our plans?' Candy asked miserably.

George did not answer this question. He said, 'I'll work for a month. Then I'll take my fifty dollars' pay and stay in a brothel all night. Or I'll sit in a bar and drink whisky until everybody goes home. Then I'll come back and work for another month, and I'll have another fifty dollars.'

Candy said, 'Lennie's such a nice fellow. I didn't think he'd do anything like this.'

George was still staring at Curley's wife. 'Lennie didn't do this because he's cruel,' he said. 'He's done a lot of bad things, but he's not a cruel man.'

George stood up and looked at Candy. 'Now listen. We've got to tell the men. They've got to catch Lennie, I suppose. There's no other way. Maybe they won't hurt him. I won't let them hurt him. Now listen carefully. The men might think I helped to kill Curley's wife, so I'm going into the bunk-house. In a minute I want you to go out and tell the men about her. Then I'll come out and pretend that I haven't seen her. Will you do that for me?'

'Of course, George,' said Candy. 'Of course I'll do that for you.'

'O.K.,' said George. 'Wait two minutes, then run out and tell the men that you've just found her. I'm going now.'

George turned and went quickly out of the barn.

Candy watched George go. Then he looked helplessly at Curley's wife. 'You're a real whore,' he said fiercely. 'You made Lennie kill you and I suppose you're glad. Everybody knew that you'd make trouble. You were no good and you're no good now, you whore.'

Candy started crying, and his voice shook. 'I could have worked in the garden on that ranch,' he continued sadly. 'And I could have washed the dishes for Lennie and George.'

Tears filled Candy's eyes as he spoke. Then he turned and went sadly out of the barn.

Outside, the noise of the horseshoe competition stopped. The sound of running feet came towards the barn, and the men rushed in: Slim, Carlson, Whit and Curley, with Crooks behind them. Candy came in after them, and George last of all. The men ran to the end of the barn. They found Curley's wife there, stopped and looked at her.

Slim went quickly to her and felt her wrist. He touched her cheek with one of his fingers, and then he put his hand under her head, feeling her broken neck. When he stood up, the other men moved towards the dead girl and stared at her.

Suddenly Curley realised what had happened. 'I know who killed her,' he cried. 'It was that big swine. I know he did it. All the other men were outside playing horseshoes.'

Curley became wild with anger. 'I'm going to get him,' he shouted. 'I'm going to fetch my shotgun and I'll kill the swine myself! I'll shoot him in the stomach. Come on, you men!' He ran quickly out of the barn.

'I'll get my pistol,' said Carlson and he ran out too.

Slim turned quietly to George. 'I suppose Lennie must have done it,' he said. 'Her neck's broken. Lennie could have done that.'

George did not answer, but he nodded slowly. His hat was pulled down on his forehead and his eyes were covered.

Slim sighed. 'Well, I suppose we've got to go and find him,' he said. 'Where do you think he went?'

George took a long time to speak. 'He'll have gone south,' he said at last. 'We came from the north, so he'll have gone south.'

'I suppose we've got to find him,' Slim repeated.

George moved closer to Slim. 'Do you think we could catch Lennie and have him put in prison?' he asked. 'He's mad, Slim. I'm sure he didn't mean to kill the girl.'

Slim nodded. 'We might be able to do that,' he said. 'We might, if we could stop Curley. But Curley will want to shoot him. Curley hasn't forgotten how Lennie broke his hand.'

'I know,' said George. 'I know.'

Carlson came running in. 'The dirty swine has stolen my pistol,' he shouted. 'It isn't in my bag.'

After Carlson came Curley, carrying a shotgun. He was calm now.

'All right, you men,' Curley said. 'Crooks has got a shotgun. Take it, Carlson. When you see Small, don't give him a chance to escape. Shoot at his stomach. That'll make him fall.'

Whit said excitedly, 'I haven't got a gun.'

Curley said, 'Whit, I want you to go to Soledad and get the sheriff. Let's go now.' He turned suspiciously to George. 'You're coming with us,' he said to him.

'Yes,' said George. 'I'll come. But listen, Curley. The poor fool's mad. Don't shoot him. He didn't know what he was doing.'

'Don't shoot him?' cried Curley. 'He's got Carlson's pistol. Of course we'll shoot him.'

George said, 'Maybe Carlson lost his pistol.'

'No,' said Carlson, 'I saw it this morning. Somebody has taken it.'

Slim stood looking down at Curley's wife. He said, 'Curley, maybe you should stay here with your wife.'

Curley's face turned red and he was furious again. 'I'm going,' he said. 'I'm going to shoot that big swine. I'm going to get him!'

Slim turned to Candy. 'Will you stay here with her then, Candy?' he said. 'The rest of us have got to go now.'

Candy nodded and the men moved away. George stopped for a moment beside Candy, and they both looked down at the dead girl. Then George moved slowly after the other men, sadly dragging his feet.

After they had gone, Candy sat down in the hay and looked at the dead girl's face. 'Poor fool,' he said softly.

The sound of the other men died away into the distance. In the barn it was gradually getting dark and the horses moved around, rattling their chains. Old Candy lay down in the hay, covered his eyes with his arm and wept quietly.

FIFTEEN

BACK TO THE POOL

In the late afternoon, the deep green pool of the Salinas River was still. The sun was shining on the tops of the Gabilan mountains, but in the valley it was getting dark.

Suddenly Lennie appeared out of some trees near the pool. He went quietly to the edge of the pool, knelt down and drank, hardly touching the water with his lips. A little bird made a noise and Lennie quickly raised his head to see where the sound was coming from. When he saw that it was only a bird, he lowered his head and drank some more water.

When he had finished, he sat down on the bank with his side to the pool. He kept looking to see if anybody came along the path. Lennie put his arms around his knees and spoke softly to himself, 'I didn't forget what to do; oh no, I didn't forget George's words. "Hide in the trees and wait for George." '

Lennie pulled his hat down over his eyes. 'George is going

to become angry with me,' he continued. 'George is going to wish he was alone, without me causing trouble for him.'

Lennie turned his head and looked at the bright mountain tops. 'I can go away up there and find a cave,' he continued sadly. 'If George doesn't want me . . . I'll go away. Yes, I'll go away.'

'I think I'll go away now,' he said. 'George isn't going to let me look after the rabbits now.'

Suddenly there was the sound of footsteps on the path. Lennie looked up and saw George walking towards him.

Lennie got up on his knees. 'You aren't going to leave me, are you, George?' he asked. 'I know you aren't.'

Walking slowly and carefully, George came closer and sat down next to Lennie. 'No,' he answered.

'I knew you wouldn't,' cried Lennie. 'You wouldn't do anything like that.'

George was silent.

'George,' said Lennie.

'Yes?'

'I've done another bad thing.'

'That doesn't make any difference,' said George, and he was silent again.

Only the tops of the mountains were lit by the sun now and the shadow in the valley was blue and soft. From the distance came the sound of men's voices.

'George,' said Lennie again.

'Yes?'

'Aren't you going to get angry with me, George?'

'Get angry?'

'Yes,' said Lennie. 'You know what you always say to me. You say, "If I didn't have you, I'd take my fifty dollars. . . ."'

'My God, Lennie!' cried George. 'You can't remember anything that happens, but you remember every word I say.'

'Well, aren't you going to say it?' asked Lennie.

George tried to repeat the well-known words. 'If I lived alone, I could have a really good time,' he said, but his voice had no interest in it. 'I could get a job without any trouble.' George stopped speaking.

'Go on,' said Lennie. 'And at the end of the month . . .'

'And at the end of the month I could take my fifty dollars and go into town and enjoy myself.' George stopped again.

Lennie looked eagerly at him. 'Go on, George,' he said. 'Aren't you going to be angry with me any more?'

'No,' said George.

'Well, I can go away,' said Lennie. 'I'll go to the hills and find a cave if you don't want me.'

Again George tried to say what Lennie was expecting. 'No,' he said. 'I want you to stay here with me.'

Now Lennie wanted to hear about other things. 'Tell me,' he said.

'Tell you what, Lennie?'

'About the other men and about us.'

'Men like us have no family and no home,' George began. 'They work for some money and then they spend it all. They've got nobody in the world to look after them. . . .'

'But not us,' Lennie cried happily. 'Tell me about us now.'

George was quiet for a moment.

'We're different,' he continued, 'because I've got you and . . .'

'And I've got you!' added Lennie happily. 'We've got each other and we look after each other.'

The gentle evening wind blew across the river and through the trees. The leaves shook and little waves flowed up the green pool. Again there was the noise of men's voices, this time much closer than before.

George took his hat off. He said nervously, 'Take your hat off, Lennie. The air feels fine.'

Lennie took off his hat and put it on the ground in front of him. The shadow in the valley was bluer than before and the evening was approaching fast. The wind carried the sound of men rushing through the trees and leaves towards them.

'Tell me how it's going to be,' said Lennie.

George had been listening to the distant sounds. For a moment he concentrated on what he was going to do. 'Look across the river, Lennie,' he said, 'and I'll tell you.'

Lennie turned his head and looked across the pool at the darkening Gabilan mountains. Then George began to speak again. 'We're going to get a little ranch,' George began. He put his hand into his side pocket and brought out Carlson's pistol. He held it in his hand on the ground behind Lennie's back, and then looked at the back of Lennie's head.

A man's voice shouted in the distance by the river, and another man answered.

'Go on,' said Lennie. 'Tell me about the ranch.'

George raised the pistol, but his hand shook, so he lowered it to the ground again.

'Go on,' said Lennie again. 'Tell me how it's going to be. We're going to get a little ranch.'

'We'll have a cow,' said George. 'And perhaps we'll have a pig and some chickens . . . and near the house we'll have an alfalfa field.'

'For the rabbits,' Lennie shouted.

'For the rabbits,' George repeated.

'And I'm going to look after the rabbits.'

'And you're going to look after the rabbits,' George repeated.

Lennie laughed happily. 'And we're going to live, really live,' he said.

'Yes.'

Lennie turned his head.

'No, Lennie,' said George. 'Look across the river and try to imagine you can see the ranch.'

Lennie obeyed him. George looked down at the pistol.

Now George could hear footsteps running through the nearby trees. George turned and looked towards them.

'Go on, George,' said Lennie once more. 'When are we going to the ranch?'

'We're going there soon.'

'You and I, together,' said Lennie.

'Yes, together,' said George. 'Everybody's going to be kind to you. There won't be any more trouble. Nobody will hurt anybody and nobody will steal anything from anybody.'

Lennie said, 'I thought you were angry with me, George.'

'No,' said George, 'I'm not angry. I've never been angry with you, Lennie, and I'm not angry now. That's something I want you to understand.'

Now the men's voices were very close. George listened to them and raised the pistol.

'Let's do it now,' Lennie said. 'Let's get that ranch now.'

'Of course,' said George. 'We'll do it now.'

George raised the pistol, held it steadily and pointed it at the back of Lennie's head. His hand started to shake violently, but then he knew what he had to do and his hand became steady again. He pulled the trigger. The sound of the shot could be heard through the whole valley. Lennie's body shook heavily, and then he fell slowly on to the sand and lay there without moving.

George shivered and looked at the pistol, then he threw it away as far as he could.

The nearby trees seemed to be full of shouting and the sound of running feet. Slim's voice shouted, 'George! Where are you, George?'

But George stayed on the bank. He sat quite still and looked at his hand that had thrown the pistol away. The men appeared and ran towards him, with Curley at the front.

Curley saw Lennie lying on the sand. 'By God, you got him,' he said. He looked down at Lennie, and then he looked back at George. 'Right in the back of the head,' Curley said quietly.

Slim went to George and sat down very close to him. 'Never mind,' said Slim. 'Sometimes a man has got to do certain things.'

But then Carlson asked George, 'How did you do it?'

'I just did it,' said George. His voice sounded very tired.

'Did he have my pistol?'

'Yes. He had your pistol,' replied George.

'And did you take it from him and kill him?' asked Carlson.

'Yes. That's how I did it.' George's voice was almost a whisper. He was still looking at his right hand that had held the pistol.

Slim touched George's shoulder. 'Come on, George,' he said. 'We'll go into town and have a drink.'

George let Slim help him to stand up.

'You had to do it, George,' said Slim. 'You had to do it. Come with me now.' He led George to the path and away towards the road to Soledad.

POINTS FOR UNDERSTANDING

CHAPTER 1

1. Why was George carrying Lennie's work card as well as his own?
2. Why did George tell Lennie that he must keep quiet when they met the boss?
3. Why did Lennie's mice always die?

CHAPTER 2

1. Why did George and Lennie have to run away from Weed?
2. Why did George want to give Lennie a puppy?
3. Why were George and Lennie not like other men who worked on ranches?
4. Lennie asked George: 'Tell me about the garden and the rabbits in the cages.' What garden and what rabbits was Lennie talking about?
5. What did George tell Lennie to do if he got into trouble?

CHAPTER 3

1. The boss asked George: 'What are you trying to hide?' What was George trying to hide from the boss?
2. Why was Curley not afraid of losing his job?
3. What did the old man think of Curley's wife?

CHAPTER 4

1. Why did George expect trouble?
2. Was Lennie attracted to Curley's wife?
3. What did George plan to do as soon as they had saved a few dollars?

CHAPTER 5

1. What did George tell Slim about Lennie's strength?
2. 'Ask him now, George,' he insisted. What did Lennie want George to ask about?
3. Who was Curley looking for?

CHAPTER 6

1. Why did George stop playing jokes on Lennie?
2. Why had Lennie been unable to let go of the girl's dress?
3. What had the men in Weed wanted to do to Lennie?
4. Why did George tell Lennie to take the puppy back to its nest?

CHAPTER 7

1. Why did Carlson think it was best to shoot Candy's old dog?
2. How did Carlson kill Candy's old dog?

CHAPTER 8

1. What was Lennie doing in the barn?
2. Why did George tell Whit that he thought there was going to be trouble?

CHAPTER 9

1. Why did Slim tell Lennie to stop stroking the puppies?
2. George and Lennie were planning a dream house. What was Lennie going to look after in this house?
3. What suggestion did Candy make to George and Lennie?
4. Why did Candy feel guilty about the way his dog had been killed?

CHAPTER 10

1. Why had Curley and Slim been quarrelling?
2. Why did Curley suddenly become angry with Lennie?
3. Slim said to Curley: 'We're going to say that your hand was trapped in a machine.' What does this tell us about the strength of Lennie's hand?

CHAPTER 11

1. Why was Crooks such a lonely man?
2. Crooks said that two things always stopped men getting land of their own. What were they?
3. How do we know that Crooks finally began to believe Lennie and Candy?

CHAPTER 12

1. How do we know that Curley's wife was not really looking for Curley?
2. Curley's wife said: 'What a husband!' Did she like her husband?
3. Life on a ranch could be very lonely. Which three lonely people have we met in the story so far?

CHAPTER 13

1. How had Lennie's puppy died?
2. Why was Curley's wife so eager to talk to Lennie?
3. Why did Curley's wife ask Lennie to stroke her hair?
4. How did Lennie try to stop Curley's wife screaming?
5. Where was Lennie going?

CHAPTER 14

1. 'Then – is that the end of our plans?' How did George reply to Candy's question?
2. George said: 'We came from the north, so he'll have gone south.' Was George telling the truth?
3. What did Carlson think had happened to his pistol? From what you know of Lennie do you think this is likely?

CHAPTER 15

1. Who had taken Carlson's pistol?
2. In Chapter 9, Candy told George: 'I shouldn't have let a stranger shoot my dog.' Why does the ending of this story make us think again of Candy's words?

GLOSSARY

SECTION 1

List of adverbs

A lot of adverbs are used in this story. If you are not sure of their meanings look them up in a dictionary. The page numbers given after the following adverb refers to the page on which it first occur.

absolutely (page 51)
coldly (page 5)
delightedly (page 8)
eagerly (page 21)
excitedly (page 24)
fiercely (page 21)
gradually (page 9)
greedily (page 1)
harshly (page 15)
helplessly (page 44)
honestly (page 21)
hopefully (page 30)

hopelessly (page 32)
innocently (page 5)
miserably (page 5)
nervously (page 3)
reluctantly (page 5)
restlessly (page 53)
sharply (page 1)
stiffly (page 32)
suspiciously (page 27)
thoughtfully (page 23)
threateningly (page 24)
violently (page 16)

SECTION 2

Idiomatic phrases

bet – I bet she does the same with Crooks (page 35)
    I'm sure . . . I'm certain. . . .
heart – know a story by heart (page 8)
    know a story from memory.
nothing – It was nothing (page 25)
    it was no trouble.

Ranch terms

agency – work card from the agency (page 3)

The owners of ranches were always looking for men to work on the ranches, but the ranches were far from the towns. The agencies were offices in towns which kept lists of ranches where workers were needed. The agencies gave the workers cards so that the owners would know which agency had sent the men.

alfalfa (page 39)

a common plant in the USA which makes good food for animals.

barley – pick up barley (page 14)

to bring the barley in from the fields when it is ripe.

denim (page 1)

a very strong cloth. There is a lot of rough work on a ranch and the men who work there have clothes made of denim.

harness – harness room (page 48)

the room where everything needed for horses is kept.

harvest the crop (page 40)

to gather the corn and barley when it is ripe.

horseshoes – a game of horseshoes (page 25)

see illustration on page 26.

machine – threshing machine (page 22)

a large machine used to separate the good part of the corn or barley from the rest.

ranch (page 3)

a farm.

team – grain team (page 14)

a number of men who work in the fields together gathering the grain crop when it is ripe.

time-book (page 13)

a notebook in which the boss wrote down the times when men began and finished work.

triangle (page 24)

a piece of metal shaped like a triangle. It is beaten with a metal bar and its noise tells the men their food is ready.

SECTION 4

Insulting words

The meanings of these terms are given below, but they are often used simply as insults and not in their particular meaning.

idiot (page 27)
> a foolish, unintelligent person.

nigger (page 18)
> an insulting word for a negro.

swine (page 17)
> a word for a pig.

tramps (page 57)
> men who have no homes and wander around from place to place begging for food and money.

whore (page 17)
> a woman who is ready to let any man make love to her – usually for money.

SECTION 5

Other words

brothel (page 39)
> a house where whores do their business. Men go there and pay money to make love to the whores.

fellow (page 12)
> a man.

ketchup (page 6)
> a thick tomato sauce.

rape (page 29)
> to attack a woman and force her to make love.

BOOKS BY
JOHN STEINBECK
(unsimplified)

FICTION
The Pearl
The Wayward Bus
Cannery Row
The Moon is Down
The Grapes of Wrath
The Long Valley
The Red Pony
Of Mice and Men
Saint Katy the Virgin
In Dubious Battle
Tortilla Flat
To a God Unknown
The Pastures of Heaven
Cup of Gold
East of Eden
Sweet Thursday
The Short Reign of Pippin IV
The Winter of Our Discontent

GENERAL
A Russian Journal
Bombs Away
Sea of Cortez (in collaboration with Edward F. Ricketts)
The Forgotten Village (documentary)
The Log from the Sea of Cortez
Once There Was A War
Travels with Charley
America and Americans

PLAYS
The Moon is Down
Of Mice and Men
Burning Bright